SCOTCH

SEVENTH EDITION

The Whisky of Scotland in Fact and Story

Sir Robert Bruce Lockhart

Preface by Robin Bruce Lockhart

Neil Wilson Publishing • Glasgow • Scotland

First published 1951
Seventh edition published 1995. Reprinted March 1996, June 1996
Neil Wilson Publishing Ltd
Suite 303a The Pentagon Centre
36 Washington Street
GLASGOW G3 8AZ
Tel: 0141 221 1117
Fax: 0141 221 5363
E-Mail: *nwp@cqm.co.uk*
http://www.nwp.co.uk/

Typeset in 12/13pt Galliard by
The Write Stuff, Glasgow. Tel: 0141 339 8279
E-mail: *wilson_i@cqm.co.uk*

Printed by Cromwell Press,
Melksham, Wilts., England

Contents

Preface

MUCH has happened in the world of whisky since the sixth edition of my late father's book *Scotch* was published. As in the case of that edition, I write this preface with both sorrow and pleasure. Sad I am that my father is no longer with us to write it himself but pleased to have the opportunity to pay tribute to a book which has become a 'classic' around the world and is as noble in many ways as Scotch whisky itself.

Although an inveterate traveller the world over my father's heart lay truly in the Highlands of Scotland and it was to Speyside, the kingdom of whisky, that he would return again and again. It was in the river Spey, near Cromdale, where my great-great-grandfather founded the Balmenach Distillery in 1824, that I scattered my father's ashes after his death in 1970.

Like my father before me, I have been a keen fisherman and for me fishing and whisky have gone together hand in hand. As a teenager I took my first salmon on the River Aven, a tributary of the Spey and it was fitting that this should have been on Haig family water. As my father did in his lifetime, I have fished the River Spey many times and sampled many of the malt whiskies in the area. I recall the inn on Grantown-on-Spey which boasted 100 different malt whiskies on its shelves.

Much of my fishing has also been done in Sutherland: the River Oykell for salmon, Loch Stack for sea trout and Loch Craggie, which used to belong to a great family friend of ours, renowned for its brown trout. The standard tipple at the end of the day was Glenmorangie from the distillery in nearby Tain. In Gaelic, Glenmorangie means 'Glen of Tranquillity'; but in the bottle it brings more than tranquillity — rather a joyous, happy, peace. Macdonald and Muir's Tain distillery celebrated its 150th anniversary in 1993 with Glenmorangie being the second-largest selling malt whisky in the United Kingdom and the fourth largest worldwide.

I thoroughly agree with my father that the true connoisseur of Scotch whisky will always choose a malt whisky but it is an invidious task to single out any particular malt as the best. Some 15 years ago, I served on a Consumer's Association *Which?* panel blind-tasting some dozen different malts. On the choice of the top three to four malts, the panel members were surprisingly close to unanimity. I refrain from citing the order in which we placed them; suffice to say, in alphabetical order, they were Glenfiddich, Glenmorangie, Macallan and Smith's Glenlivet. Perhaps it is not a coincidence that these four malts, along with Glen Grant, acquired by Seagrams as part of the Glenlivet Distilleries group in 1978, were the top-selling five malt whiskies in the United Kingdom and in the world as a whole in 1993. With the exception of Glenmorangie, all come from Speyside distilleries.

Glenfiddich, the top-selling malt in the United Kingdom, is produced by William Grant & Sons Ltd which was established in 1887. In the late 1950s, my father, along with Sir Compton Mackenzie of *Whisky Galore* fame, appeared in a series of nationwide advertisements for Grant's whisky. Macallan — a favourite of mine — was legally established in 1824 when new laws allowed the production of whisky to go 'legal'. Smith's Glenlivet, usually referred to as 'The Glenlivet', and my great-great-grandfather's Balmenach Distillery were legalised at the same time. Along with many others they had been producing illicitly distilled whisky for generations.

In addition to Macallan's sales to the general public, its malt also forms an important part of such well-known blended whiskies as Ballantine's, Chivas Regal, Cutty Sark, The Famous Grouse, J & B Rare and other leading blends. Balmenach malt has been part of the make-up of Johnnie Walker Black Label for untold years.

There are many other excellent malt whiskies I could mention but most are solely or largely used for blending or export only. Nevertheless, I must make mention of Laphroaig, a product of Allied Distillers, coming from the island of Islay. Its peaty flavour is very different from that of most other malts and so it is not strictly comparable. To some, Laphroaig is an acquired taste; I will only say that once acquired it is something possessed for ever.

I note with pleasure that the volume of world sales of bottled malt whisky has risen 500% since 1975, the majority of this increase coming from exports. Yet sales of bottled malt whisky are only some 10% of total Scotch whisky sales. The remaining 90% consists of the sale of blended whisky. The amount of malt whisky in blended whisky varies, but is usually between 35% and 40%. So, in effect, the total output from distilleries is about 50% malt and 50% grain.

A seventh edition of *Scotch* had been planned for publication in 1987 but the enormity of the financial scandals surrounding the bitter Guinness take-over battle for Distillers Co. Ltd (DCL), which began in 1986 and ended in several prominent City tycoons receiving jail sentences and/or heavy fines, resulted in a decision to postpone publication. The legal wrangles were continuing and the dangers of publishing libellous material were very real. Curiously, the take-over battle started exactly 100 years after DCL first obtained a share quotation on the London Stock Exchange. Subsequently, Guinness made a multi-million pound out-of-court settlement to Argyll Securities, the other bidder for DCL, and today, not one member of the present Guinness main board of directors held office at the time of the take-over.

The Guinness subsidiary, United Distillers, today has a 37% share of world volume sales of Scotch whisky, virtually all blended whiskies. Although United Distillers owns just over 30% of Highland malt distilleries, only 1% of production is sold as malt, the rest goes into blending. In 1993, sales of Johnnie Walker Red Label, United Distillers' world best-seller, sold over six million cases; these, together with a sale of over four million cases of Johnnie Walker Black Label, meant that Johnnie Walker sales topped 10 million cases for the first time.

The world's second most popular blended whisky is J & B Rare, produced by Justerini & Brooks, a subsidiary of Grand Metropolitan. J & B Rare contains a higher proportion of malt whisky than most blends with over 35 different malts going into the blending. Sales have risen 800% since the mid-1960s with over 95% sold in the export market. Third in the league of blended whisky exports comes Allied Distillers' Ballantine's.

Apart from acquiring one of the most famous of malt distilleries, Glenlivet — Seagram, the large Canadian distiller, bought the old established Chivas Brothers at an earlier date — 1949. The brothers' partnership was formed in 1858 and was soon involved in the whisky trade, including the export market. By 1909, the company had introduced Chivas Regal, which is the top de-luxe brand worldwide, marketed in over 150 countries.

Another very prominent blended whisky in the export trade is Cutty Sark — a top seller in the United States. First produced in 1923 by the wine merchants Berry Brothers & Rudd, it soon established itself across the Atlantic in Prohibition times. The legendary Prohibition gangster Jack 'Legs' Diamond once called at Berry's shop in London in the 1930s to place an order and removed a consignment in a fleet of taxis. An unusual beginning for a brand leader!

The origins of distilling in Scotland are lost in the mists of time, perhaps dating back 2000 years or more. Nevertheless, 1994 was celebrated as the 500th anniversary of the official existence of Scotch whisky. The first written record of it can be found in the Scottish Exchequer Roll of 1494. Today whisky is the favourite tipple of countless millions throughout the world. Even in France — a country normally somewhat xenophobic when it comes to foreign drink — more whisky is drunk in a month than cognac in a year.

My regret — and one which I know my father would have shared with me were he alive — is that the profit motive of some producers has resulted in cheaper but inferior whisky reaching retailers' shelves both at home and abroad.

Except for some alterations and updating of statistics in the last chapter *Whisky Now*, I have left the 1981 edition of my father's book relatively unchanged. This essentially preserves the book as a work which observed the workings and development of the industry after the Second World War. To have revised his conclusions would destroy the integrity of a book which gives the reader valuable insights into the world of Scotch whisky at a particular stage in its development. I leave you with one thought to muse over. When I served on the *Which?* tasting panel to which I have already referred, this was just one panel of a number organised by *Which?* to cover all types of wines and spirits produced in the main countries of the world. At the end of all these tastings *Which?* made the observation that the malt whisky panel was much more cheerful than any of the others!

For help in preparation of my new preface and for the statistical updating in the last chapter, my fullest thanks to the Scotch Whisky Association, Guinness plc, Seagram Distillers plc, William Grant & Sons Ltd, Macallan-Glenlivet plc, Macdonald & Muir Ltd, Allied Distillers Ltd, Justerini & Brooks Ltd, Berry Brothers & Rudd Ltd, and for financial background information, the stockbrokers Barclays de Zoete Wedd.

Robin Bruce Lockhart
Hove, Sussex
January, 1995

PART I

The Water of Life

CHAPTER ONE

The Origins

INSPIRING, BOLD JOHN BARLEYCORN,
WHAT DANGERS THOU CANST MAKE US SCORN.

BURNS

THIS book is a personal history of Scotch whisky. My qualifications for writing it are perhaps slender, for I am no technical expert. All I can say is that I spent the happiest days of my youth at Balmenach, one of the oldest licensed malt distilleries in the Highlands. Situated near the former Royal Burgh of Cromdale, today a tiny village close to the River Spey, it belonged for over a century to my mother's family. My Macgregor great-grand-father, who began life as a poor crofter, built it, and every year, unless I am kept abroad, I return to it with the hom-ing instinct which lies so deep in the heart of the wandering Scot. The link with the past has perhaps a stronger hold on Scots than on any other race, and I share to the full this romantic attachment of my countrymen. Although my father was a Lowlander, the Celtic blood is the dominant in my veins. Whisky has made and unmade four generations of Macgregors. I have drunk it and seen it drunk in many parts of the world, and I am unrepentant.

Today there are many varieties of whisky and many

countries have tried to make it. Indeed, spirit classed as whisky can now be manufactured anywhere, but should be made from no other materials than malt and unmalted grain. Six types of whisky predominate.

Pride of place belongs to Scotch malt whisky which is distilled in Scotland in a simple pot-still from a mash *consisting entirely of malted barley*. It has a more distinctive flavour than all other whiskies owing to the exclusive use of malted barley and to the design of the stills.

Scotch grain whisky is distilled in a 'patent' or continuous still from a mixed mash of cereal grain, preferably maize. Malted barley is used to convert or saccharify the unmalted grain used in the mash. The grain 'patent-still' has a more efficient rectification and greater fuel economy, but the whisky has less character than Scotch 'malt'.

Blended Scotch whisky is a mixture of matured Scotch 'malt' and Scotch 'grain'. The character of the blend is influenced partly by the skill and judgment of the blender and partly by the quality of the whiskies used.

Irish whiskey is distilled in Ireland from a mash of cereal grains saccharified by malted grain.

American rye whiskey is made from a mash of mixed cereal grains. The mash must contain at least 51% of rye.

American Bourbon or corn whiskey is distilled from a mash which must contain 51% of maize.

To make the distinction clear, American whiskey should be labelled rye whiskey or grain whiskey.

The best malt whisky was and is still made in the Highlands of Scotland and supplies the essential character to the numerous brands of blended Scotch which, on account of their lighter nature have found the highest favour with the urban population of the whisky-drinking world. Scotch malt is a he-man's drink and goes with hard toil and strenuous exercise in the open air. Blended Scotch is for weaker stomachs.

The very word whisky is Celtic and comes from the Gaelic *uisge-beatha* which means the water of life and, for better or worse, but mostly, I think, for better, it has been to the Gaels what wine is to the Latin races of the Mediterranean. It is, too, or was, until English taxation put it beyond reach of the humble man, essentially the drink of the people. The Lowland gentry and at least some of the Highland lairds drank claret, but, as Scott rightly says, the character of a nation is not to be learnt from its fine folks. The history of malt whisky lies shrouded in the mists of the Celtic dawn, and abler and more romantic pens than mine have tried to unveil the mysteries of its origin. Some romantic writers have gone even so far as to claim that *uisge-beatha* was the tipple of Noah and that Dionysos was the god of whisky before he was the god of wine! Other authorities hold that wise men in the East discovered that cereals and spirits were the secret of long life and that the Celts simplified the recipe by combining the two in whisky. Stronger evidence of the antiquity of malt whisky can be found in classical allusions to the distillation or brewage from barley made by the ancient Egyptians and called by the Greeks barley-wine. What is certain is that the Egyptians still make whisky today. Known as *bolonachi,* it was bought eagerly by our troops in the Middle East during the last war and, *pace* Field-Marshal Montgomery, played its part in the victory of El Alamein.

I think it probable that whisky came to Scotland from Ireland, was first manufactured in the west, and then found its way to the Central Highlands and the chosen land between the Cairngorms and the Moray Firth. Be this as it may, it is a fact that for centuries a spirit distilled from a fermented barley mash has been made all over the Highlands where Nature still supplies the essential ingredients for its distillation: home-grown barley for the malt, the pure air of the mountains, the unpolluted water of the hill burns, the rich dark peat of the moor, and, in the opinion of some experts, the granite rocks from which the water springs. Even in these modern days of blended whisky there are distillers who claim that the best malt whisky comes 'off granite through peat'. What is certain is that 'off peat through granite' produces a different taste. No two malt whiskies are, in fact, alike. Distillation means 'to extract the essence of', and the essence is never the same. The best malt whisky is a noble drink fit to be compared with the finest brandy. To some Highlanders it is still the only Scotch whisky and until well on into the nineteenth century every Highlander knew how to make it. To him it was in its literal sense the water of life, and as late as 1800 the *Catholic Register* mentions Tomintoul as a place where 'everyone made whisky and everyone drank it'. It is almost the first reference in history to the little mountain village from which my Macgregor forebears crossed the Cromdale hills in order to settle at Balmenach.

This Highland knowledge of pot-still distillation was not without its dangers. As a young boy I remember vividly the shock I received on reading R. M. Ballantyne's *The Lonely Island*. The book was a Christmas present, and I read it in two days. The lonely island was Pitcairn Island, and the book told the story of the life of the *Bounty* mutineers who found asylum there. It is a tale written for boys, and adorned with a typically Victorian moral. At first the little community thrives under the leadership of Fletcher Christian. True it is that the mutineers took unto themselves native wives, but in all other respects the Bible was their guide and mentor. No boys' book of those days was complete without at least one villain. *The Lonely Island* has two: Quintal and McCoy. One night Quintal goes to McCoy's hut and finds him gloating over a kettle with a twisted pipe and exclaiming: 'Ha, ha, I've got it at last.'

'Long and earnestly,' writes Mr Ballantyne, 'had McCoy laboured to make use of a fatal piece of knowledge which he possessed. Among the hills of Scotland he had learnt the art of making ardent spirits. After many failures, he had on this night made a successful attempt with the "ti-root" which grew in abundance on Pitcairn.'

The reader can guess the sequel. McCoy and Quintal start an all-night carousal which ends in a fight between the two men. Mr Ballantyne describes the consequences of the disastrous discovery in a chapter called 'The Darkest Hour'. In a fit of *delirium tremens* McCoy falls over a high cliff and is killed. Quintal, instead of pulling himself together, goes from bad to worse, and, finally Adams and Young, the only other remaining white men, decide to put him to death. They polish him off with an axe. Soon afterwards the gentle Young dies of consumption — tubercular and not alcoholic — and Adams, the Bible reader, is left as the sole white.

Although some of R. M. Ballantyne's stories are still read; notably *Coral Island* and *Ungava,* the vast majority of the 70-odd books which he wrote have been long forgotten, and in 1950 I had to go to the National Library in Edinburgh to find a copy of *The Lonely Island.*

I must have been 10 or 11 when I first read the book. Today it recalls the nursery rhyme of the *Ten Little Nigger Boys,* but remains in my memory as a reminder that, while whisky can be a friend in need, it is also an enemy to those who misuse its virtues.

For some strange reason whisky has always been more violently attacked than any other alcoholic drink, particularly by Scots who have combined high thinking with hard drinking and whose Presbyterian conscience suffers occasionally from the twinges of repletion. Indeed, the attitude of some Scots towards whisky is not unlike that of an old Scottish widow whose daughter Maggie had strayed from the path of virtue and had been to the court to claim an affiliation order. 'Maggie,' said the old mother, 'this'll be a lesson tae ye. It'll no' deter you from sin, but it'll rob ye o' the pleasure o' committing it.'

Although distilling is no longer part of the Highlander's natural education, the Highlands are the home of malt whisky, and they always will be; the best malt whisky is produced in the belt of land bounded on the west by the River Ness and on the east by the River Deveron. Here nature has been generous in her gifts. The land, cold and hard in winter but in summer warm to eye and heart, slopes down from the granite of the Blue Mountains through peat and heather moor to the rich farmlands which lie to the Moray Firth and which grow the life-giving barley. It is peopled by a race which retains to this day the graces and natural manners of the Highlander. Wondrously beautiful are the summer evenings when sky and setting sun weave a kaleidoscopic pattern of light and shade on hill and glen, until night in the form of a low white bank of cloud steals slowly like a wraith over the tops of Cairngorm and Braeriach.

It is a land to which any Ulysses would wish to return

after his travels, and to me it is all that is left of home. There is a magic, too, in the rivers which water it: the wild Findhorn, the noble Deveron, the lordly Spey with its numerous tributaries including the swift ice-clear Aven into which runs the world-famous Livet. Who shall say which is dearest to his heart, when each stream has its local lovers?

An Avenside poetaster, George Bruce Cumming, sings the merits of the Scottish rivers in the following verse:

The rapid Spey, the burly Tay,
Their banks are broad and braw;
The Don and Dee are fair to see,
But Aven dings* them a'.

Allowing for local patriotism, I do not dispute this verdict. On the other hand, other local enthusiasts may well object to my preference for Speyside malt whisky, and, in truth, superb malt whiskies were, and are made still, in Skye, in Islay, in Sutherland, in Caithness and in Campbeltown in Kintyre. Lowland distilleries, too, made an early appearance in the history of whisky, but no-one would seriously put forward a claim for the superlative merits of their product. Apart from Ireland — and Irish whiskey does not enter into my story — both the distillation and the drinking of whisky were confined almost entirely to Highlanders until the middle of the eighteenth century, when Lowland malt distilleries began to cater for the growing urban population.

In the Highlands the distilleries were small and supplied mainly local needs. The needs were considerable, for to the Highlander whisky was a daily necessity. It stood on the breakfast table or all day on a side table — as at Balmenach even in my lifetime — and was drunk by all the household and pressed on every caller. In his admirable little book called *Whisky*, Mr Aeneas Macdonald quotes a eulogy by an exciseman who, writing in 1736 on the manners of the Highlanders, pays this tribute to the water of life: 'The ruddy complexion, nimbleness and strength of these people is not owing to water-drinking but to the aqua vitae, a malt spirit which serves both for victual and drink.'

Because whisky was the natural drink of the Highlander

* *Beats*

and because the Highlands themselves were almost unknown territory until after the '45, the spirit made a late appearance in Scottish literature. Burns was and remains its great poet and he would, if alive today, have received a fortune for the publicity which he gave to it.

Some modern whisky experts have questioned Burns's taste and have doubted whether, in spite of being an excise officer, he knew much about the merits of good malt whisky. Be this as it may, he was well acquainted with Ferintosh, a malt whisky produced by Duncan Forbes of Culloden who, for his services to the Government, was granted the privilege of distilling it free of duty. When the privilege was withdrawn in 1784, Burns burst forth into indignant song:

> *Thee, Ferintosh! O sadly lost!*
> *Scotland, lament frae coast to coast!*
> *Now colic grips an' barkin' hoast*
> *May kill us a'.*

Certainly no poet has sung the merits of whisky so often and so well as Burns. He rated it far higher than brandy which he dismissed as 'burning trash'.

Sir Walter Scott, a connoisseur of Scottish food and drink, had a finer taste and knowledge than Burns, and both James Hogg, the Ettrick Shepherd, and he were loud in their praises of Glenlivet. Indeed, 'Christopher North' puts in Hogg's mouth an ecstatic paean: 'If a body could just find oot the exac' proper proportion and quantity that ought to be drunk every day, and keep to that, I verily trow that he might leeve for ever, without dying at a', and that doctors and kirkyards would go oot o' fashion.'

In *Catriona*, too, Stevenson makes James More Macgregor say in reply to David Balfour's statement that in the morning he drinks nothing else but spare, cold water: 'Tut-tut, that is fair destruction to the stomach, take an old campaigner's word for it. Our country spirit at home is perhaps the most entirely wholesome; but as that is not come-at-able, Rhenish or a white wine of Burgundy will be the next best.'

21

In Scottish historical records whisky is mentioned at an early date. Before 1500 it had already reached the Royal table and, as the records show, was appreciated by King James IV who fell at Flodden. Later, it gave life and energy to the soldiers of Montrose and lent them wings in those forced marches which still astonish the historians by their rapidity. In the '45 it sustained the Highlanders of Prince Charles Edward and consoled the Prince himself after the disaster of Culloden. It was, as Mr Neil Gunn has written so cogently, the Prince's short desperate adventure with whisky before he relapsed into the death of brandy.

On the grim battlefield of Culloden whisky was used, perhaps for the first time, for a sacred purpose when John Maitland, a Presbyter of the Episcopal Church of Scotland, administered the Holy Eucharist to the mortally wounded Lord Strathallan with oatcake and whisky, 'the requisite elements not being attainable'.

Culloden is the most important date in the story of whisky. It ruined the Jacobite chiefs and exalted the Whigs who had supported the Hanoverians. It also opened the Highlands to the Lowlands and the road to the South for Highland whisky. From now on whisky, instead of being what Burns called 'the poor man's wine', was to become more and more a factory product.

Although a duty of 2d. a gallon had been imposed on whisky as far back as 1660, the Highlander paid no attention to it. Culloden was to bring in its train an invasion of excisemen, known locally as gaugers, because in early days they had to gauge the malt to assess the duty, and a mass of crippling legislation including a rise in the duty. Again the Highlanders ignored the attempts of the Government to control their national drink. In defiance of the law they started a smuggling trade which expanded rapidly with a demand for Scotch whisky in England and the imposition of an import duty of 9s. 6d. per gallon by the English Government. At one period, of which I shall have more to say in a later chapter, there was almost open warfare. Illicit stills flourished, and at first the Government were powerless to suppress them. In 1814 all distillation in the Highlands in stills of less than 500 gallons was prohibited. In 1823 there were myriad charges of illicit distillation, but the smuggling trade continued unabated, and at this time more than half the whisky sold came from the illicit distilleries in the Highlands. Profit was not by any means the only motive. The Highlanders, embittered by defeat, were determined not only to defend what they considered their rights but also to prevent the English Government from suppressing the remaining fragments of Gaelic civilisation. And for any Sassenach to doubt that malt whisky is an essential part of Gaelic civilisation is proof that he totally misunderstands the Highlander's attitude towards his national drink.

The resistance of the Highlanders had one vital influence on the fate of whisky. By general acknowledgment the best whisky was made in those parts of the Highlands which had suffered most from the defeat of the Jacobites. Among the numerous harsh measures by which the Government sought to tame the Highlanders the ban on the small stills and the duty on whisky were bitterly resented. The law was openly defied, and the Highlander continued to make illegally the spirit in small stills which English legislators had decided should be made in stills of not less than 500 gallons. Consumers wanted Highland whisky, and the smugglers saw that they got it. By so doing, they maintained the quality of malt whisky and kept alive the traditions of its distillation. It is, therefore, fitting that Glenlivet, the centre of the smugglers' war, should be today the most famous whisky in the world.

This illegal persistence on the part of the Highlander was of great benefit to the good name of 'Scotch', for, with the increased demand for whisky, illicit stilling in Lowland cities like Edinburgh soon developed on a large scale. The whisky was of dubious quality, and, more often than not, went raw from the illicit still to the urban consumer in whose eyes its only merit was its cheapness. The flesh of the impoverished townsman was weak and the spirit was strong.

By 1820 illicit distilling had become so widespread that, in order to check this lawlessness and to restore the pre-eminence of Highland whisky, the Duke of Gordon raised the matter in the House of Lords. As the largest landowner in the Central Highlands he was well-qualified to speak. He told the peers that nothing could stop the Highlander from making and selling whisky, but that if the Government would sanction the manufacture of legal whisky of a quality equal to the illicit on a payment of a reasonable duty, he and the other Highland landowners would do their best to suppress smuggling.

His proposal was approved, and the Act of 1823 sanctioned legal distilling on payment of a duty of 2s. 3d. per gallon of proof spirit and a licence of £10 for all stills with a capacity of 40 gallons and over.

The Act has an important place in the history of whisky. It encouraged the production of good whisky at the expense of the fire-water of the illicit stills of the cities and, by so doing, favoured the Highlands where Nature has always meant real Scotch to be produced.

Illicit distilling, however, continued fairly widely for 60 years and it was not until the English took to whisky and, to meet their taste, blending came into fashion, that it virtually ceased. That up to 1850 and even later whisky was still drunk mainly by Scots is proved by the report on the drinking habits of Scotland issued in 1842 by the Committee of the General Assembly of the Established Church. In 1842 England with a population of 15,000,000 consumed 7,956,054 gallons of spirit (mainly brandy, gin and rum) or approximately half a gallon per mouth of population. Ireland with a population of just over 8,000,000 consumed 5,290,650 gallons; roughly two-thirds of a gallon per mouth. Scotland with a population of 3,620,184 drank 5,595,186 gallons, mostly whisky, or more than two gallons per mouth of population! It is a formidable statistic.

Malt whisky was an integral part of Scottish life and entered into its ritual. It was and, to a smaller extent, remains the only drink at weddings and the final door drink (*deoch an dorius*) to any parting guest. Even more so was it the drink *de rigueur* at every funeral of rich and poor alike. A laird would consider it a disgrace if at his mother's funeral his guests were not carried to their beds; a poor crofter would spend or borrow what he could to send the mourners away fully satisfied. Sometimes the wake started before the burial, and in a Highland village less than 70 years ago one lasted for three days until olfactory reasons compelled the mourners to remove the corpse of the departed. Today the wake has virtually ceased, although since the last war I have seen a modest one. It needed no stretch of my imagination to realise what the wakes of a century ago must have been like.

In those days the Highland women drank their share, and, as Smollett tells us in *Humphry Clinker*, whisky was given 'with great success to infants, as a cordial, in the confluent smallpox'. In at least one instance, too, malt whisky provided by a Highland lady smoothed the way to Royal favour. In 1822 King George IV visited Scotland. Arrayed in Highland dress, he would have nothing but Glenlivet whisky. In her still popular *Memoirs of a Highland Lady* Elizabeth Grant of Rothiemurchus tells how she met his need.

There was no Glenlivet in Edinburgh, let alone at Holyroodhouse, and Lord Conyngham, the Chamberlain, was in despair. Elizabeth's father, Sir John Peter Grant, sent word to his daughter who was in Rothiemurchus. Much against her will the lady, who was cellarer, emptied her pet bin 'long in wood, mild as milk, and the true contraband *goût in* it'. The King was graciously pleased to drink the whisky and to express his gratitude. A reminder of this attention at a proper moment by the grateful Chamberlain obtained for Miss Grant's father a long-sought Indian judgeship.

Although whisky, in the Highlands at any rate, is still regarded as a spirit not to be adulterated or tampered with, I must admit that there were and are recipes for its use as a medicine and also for the final glory of a feast, recipes far more ancient than the blended whisky which we drink today. Of these the best known are toddy and Atholl brose. Toddy, excellent both as a cure for cold and as an elixir of life, requires careful preparation. The ingredients are sugar, boiling water and preferably a well-matured malt whisky. First, you heat the tumbler with warm water and, when the glass has reached a comfortable temperature, you pour out the water. Then into the empty glass you put two or three squares of loaf-sugar and add enough boiling water — a wineglass should suffice — to dissolve the sugar. Then add a wineglass of whisky and stir with a silver spoon; then another wineglass of boiling water, and finally to crown this liquid edifice top it with another wineglass of whisky. Stir again and drink the contents with slow and loving care. As a cure for cold, take your toddy to bed, put one bowler hat at the foot, and drink until you see two.

This is the ordinary Scottish recipe for toddy; an alternative interpretation is that of my old Russian friend, the late M. Baleiev, who founded the famous Chauve-Souris cabaret show in Moscow and, after the Russian revolution, brought it to London and New York. Here is his version: 'First you put in whisky to make it strong; then you add water to make it weak; next you put in lemon to make it sour, then you put in sugar to make it sweet. You put in more whisky to kill the water. Then you say "Here's to you" — and you drink it yourself.'

Atholl Brose is a concoction which is drunk in company and on festive occasions like Hogmanay and St. Andrew's Day. There are various recipes, but the simplest method is to mix an equal quantity of running heather honey and fine oatmeal in a little cold water. Then, according to the number of your guests, pour in very slowly a well-flavoured malt whisky. Stir the whole contents vigorously until a generous froth rises to the top. Then bottle and cork tightly, keep for two days and serve in the finest silver bowl that you possess. A pound of oatmeal and a pound of honey will need four pints of whisky, and the quantity required can be reduced or increased in these proportions.

Atholl Brose is a giant's drink, and I have vivid memories of the St. Andrew's Day I organised in Prague, when we left the making of the brose to the Military Attaché. It was the first St. Andrew's Day dinner ever held in the Czechoslovak capital, and the M.A., a Sassenach, resolved that it should not be forgotten. For several days he worked in secret. When the brose was passed round in a magnificent loving cup with two handles, with a guest standing up on each side of the drinker, the fumes were almost overpowering. The M.A. had laced the brose with an over-generous measure of slivovice, the potent plum vodka of Slovakia. He suffered for his intervention in Scottish affairs. After the dinner there were several casualties and the only standing survivors were three Scots and Jan Masaryk.

All that remains to be told in this chapter is that Highlanders always drank their malt whisky undiluted. It was a custom eulogised and followed by a distinguished Saxon connoisseur. The late Professor Saintsbury began his *Notes on a Cellar Book* in Elgin where he was for two years a schoolmaster. In his book he records his preference for malt whisky 'single, old and neat'.

Today pure malt whisky is rare. To those who can still obtain it a little water is permissible with the whisky, but preferably after it. Soda water is an abomination and degrades both the spirit and the soul. By and large, the connoisseur still abides by the old Highland saying: 'There are two things a Highlander likes naked, and one is malt whisky.'

We shall see later that the great boom in whisky came from an invention which was to lead to an immense increase in production. It was to ensure the universal triumph of whisky and the conquest of the English and world markets. It was also to alter both the quality and the taste of the spirit.

Ironically the vast whisky fortunes were to be made, not by the original Highland distillers, but by the traders and blenders.

CHAPTER TWO

Glenlivet and the Grants

GLENLIVET IT HAS CASTLES THREE,
DRUMIN, BLAIRFINDY AND DESKIE,
AND ALSO ONE DISTILLERY,
MORE FAMOUS THAN THE CASTLES THREE.

I HAVE already made it clear that malt whisky is the original and best Scotch whisky and that in the verdict of poet and philosopher, crofter and craftsman, nobleman and ne'er-do-well, one of the finest malt whiskies is made in Glenlivet. The distillery fully justifies the doggerel verse which heads this chapter, for the castles are now ruins and Glenlivet still flourishes. Itself not beautiful, it has a superb site and stands on a pleasant brae halfway between Ballindalloch and Tomintoul in the heart of the remote and still unspoilt Banffshire Highlands.

Apart from its beauty, the glen provides all the essentials of good whisky. The fertile fields of the Laichs of Banff and Moray were made for barley. The Livet which waters the glen runs down in a sparkling limpid stream from the Cairngorms. A few miles away is the renowned Faemussach mossy moor with its almost inexhaustible deposits of the finest peat. The air makes you feel as if you were walking on the top of the world. As for the distillers, whom Scott appropriately called 'the cunning chemists', there was, towards the end of the eighteenth century, a wider knowledge of distilling in the Glenlivet-Tomintoul area than in any other part of Scotland.

Although I do not know it like Balmenach, the Glenlivet Distillery has been a landmark in my life for many years. As the centre and last stronghold of the smugglers, the glen itself has an exciting history.

In its efforts to pacify the Highlands after the '45 the British Government, by the Act of 1787, divided Scotland into Lowland and Highland districts. The object was to facilitate the collection of the duty on whisky. All the hardships of the Act fell on the unfortunate Highlanders. While England and the Scottish Lowlands continued to pay duty on each gallon of spirits, the Highlanders were charged on the capacity of the still. Moreover, the spirits produced by the Highland distillers had to be sold within the thinly populated Highland district.

These vindictive measures, applied at a time when the first demands for Scotch whisky were coming from England, provoked the smugglers' war. Illicit stills sprang up like mushrooms in the night. Favoured by its inaccessibility, Glenlivet was in the thick of the battle. Farmers left their ploughs and set up stills of which in the Glenlivet-Tomintoul area there were soon more than 200. An army of gaugers, sometimes supported by the military, invaded the country, but for a long time was unable to stem the smugglers' tide of success. The smugglers — sturdy, determined and embittered by injustice — loaded their whisky on hill-ponies and led them skilfully by secret tracks across the mountains to the rich markets of the Lowlands. 'Freedom and whisky gang taegither', wrote Burns, and the smugglers' interpretation of freedom was to defy the central authority with all their might. In modern times the French philosopher Alain was to say in almost the same words that such defiance is the sacred duty of every democratic citizen.

To a large extent the war was a long battle of wits, and here the advantage lay with the Highlanders who, moving in armed bands of 20 or 30 men, knew almost blindfold every inch of a country as suitable for smuggling as

Yugoslavia is today for guerrilla warfare. They showed, too, great ingenuity in making the gauger actually pay for their illicit trade. Somewhat stupidly the Government offered a reward of £5 to anyone who reported the whereabouts of an illicit still. In those days the most expensive part of a primitive still was the 'worm', a coiled copper pipe which condenses into liquid the hot vapour from the wash-still and then passes it into the spirit-still. When their copper pipe was worn out, the smugglers used to dismantle their still, taking good care to remove whatever might be of further use to them, but leaving the worn-out worm and other minor implements to show that a still had been there. One of the smugglers would then go to the gauger, report that he had discovered a still, and receive the £5 as a reward. With the money thus acquired the smugglers would then buy the copper for a new pipe and set up their still in another glen.

In some parts of the Highlands gauger and smuggler were on good terms although they watched one another like keeper and poacher. On one occasion a smuggler was cautioned by a gauger in a friendly manner. Both were Highlanders.

'Sandy', said the gauger, 'you and I are well acquent and ye ken I'm a man o' my word. Weel, I'm telling you for your own good. Ye're going too far, and I've my orders. From now on I'm on your trail.'

'Thanks,' says Sandy. 'Ye'll admit my word's as good as your ain. Weel, I'll gie ye a chance. On Friday I'll bring in a firkin o' whisky under your very eyes and it'll be on the North road between Beauly and Inverness between 9am and 5pm.

With much emphasis on the sanctity of the smuggler's word the two men parted, and by the Friday the gauger had gathered a strong band of excise officers and police to watch the road. From nine in the morning onwards there was a steady stream of traffic. First came carts with hay. Each cart was searched. Then came carts with turnips followed by carts with sheep, and later carts with wood. All were examined with infinite care, but no whisky was found. Later, came a funeral cortege which held up the queue of carts for some time until a dray with a load of oats made a sudden dash to pass the procession. 'Stop that dray!' said the head gauger. The dray was searched in vain.

The queue of carts continued until five in the evening when the gauger and his weary men were glad to call a halt.

Later in the evening gauger and smuggler met to compare notes, and the gauger took Sandy to task.

'It's no' the playing of a trick on me that I mind', he said. 'It's the fact that you broke your pledged word. Man, I trusted you.

'I kept my word,' said Sandy, 'and the whisky's in Inverness now.'

'Ye brought the whisky along the North road between nine and five. Have you any witnesses?'

'Aye,' says Sandy, 'there's yersel. Man, ye took off yer hat to it.'

Other encounters between gauger and smuggler were not so good-natured and sometimes led to violence. On one occasion smugglers in Glen Urquhart were about to run a big load of whisky by road along Loch Ness to Inverness when they were warned by a friend that the excise officers were on their track. The smugglers assembled an array of casks, filled with herrings, on the west side of Loch Ness and then with feigned secrecy rowed the load across to the east side. No sooner had they landed their casks than the gaugers who had been lying in wait charged. The smugglers defended their casks with vigour, and blows were exchanged and several heads broken before smugglers and casks were captured and lodged in Inverness jail. Meantime, of course, the illicit whisky, sent by road on the west side of Loch Ness, had arrived safely in the Highland capital.

The smugglers came up the next day before the Sheriff who, knowing very well that the excisemen had been hoaxed, asked the smugglers why they had not told the gaugers that the casks contained only herrings. The men pleaded that they were defending their property from a brutal attack, and the Sheriff upheld their right and acquitted them. An unfair law had all the Highlands against it, and lawlessness continued to flourish.

For toughness and disregard of life and limb the men of

Glenlivet and Tomintoul were unrivalled even in the Highlands, and John Wilson ('Christopher North'), who visited Tomintoul in 1815, described it as 'a wild mountain village where drinking, dancing, swearing and quarrelling went on all the time'. Assuredly the first poet to visit the home of my forebears, he himself did not escape an exchange of blows, for he had a fight with a local tinker. Nevertheless, the place must have put its charm on him, for he returned the next year, and in those days it was a journey for stout hearts and sturdy legs.

Among the Glenlivet farmers who fought the protracted struggle against the law was a young man called George Smith. Well educated and something of a Latin scholar, he had been trained as an architect. On his father's death, however, he took over the farm of Upper Drumin close to the village of Glenlivet. Like his neighbours he had an illicit still on his farm and took a leading part in the incessant campaign of desperate pursuits and perilous escapes which characterised the war with the gaugers.

Then came the Act of 1823 which, on the Duke of Gordon's proposal, sanctioned legal distilling on payment of a licence fee. Too shrewd to believe that the profitable smuggling trade could continue for ever, George Smith of Glenlivet thought twice. He had done well both as a distiller and as a farmer. In 1824 he decided to consolidate his gains and to take out a licence, and in the same year the Glenlivet Distillery came into official existence.

Encouraged by the Duke of Gordon, George Smith rebuilt his distillery to his own plans and set up as the first licensed distiller in Glenlivet. His decision required both moral and physical courage. Fortunately for him, he possessed both, as well as a robust and powerful frame, for his former companions in smuggling were enraged by what they considered his disloyalty and regarded him as the worst of blacklegs. For a long time they threatened to burn his new distillery, lay in wait for his whisky convoys, sometimes with success, and hustled and abused him on market days and even at kirk on Sundays. For several years he carried in his belt a pair of loaded pistols presented to him by the Laird of Aberlour and, accompanied by a band of armed servants, led his packhorses in person over the mountain tracks to Perth and Edinburgh.

The pistols, I understand, were used only once. Coming back from a successful trip to the South, George Smith stopped at a house, half-farm, half-inn, at Cockbridge, a lonely spot at the bottom of the fierce hill which descends from the highest point of the Lecht road to the upper valley of the Don. In the room into which he was shown George Smith found other travellers, brawny and fierce-looking fellows who eyed his stocky figure and, more particularly, the curious bulkiness of his waist with hostile suspicion. And, in truth, the purse-belt which George Smith wore under his clothes was heavy with gold.

Thinking preventive action better than an unequal skirmish, George Smith took out one of his loaded pistols, and, aiming at the topmost peat in the fireplace, shattered it to pieces with one shot. The men slunk from the room and left him unmolested.

These precautions were grimly necessary. Had they not been taken and had Smith himself not been a formidable personality, there would have been no Glenlivet Distillery today. The men of the glen were no chicken hearts and would have shrunk at nothing to prevent any split in the smugglers' ranks. Their temper was expressed by Burns in *Tam O'Shanter*: 'Wi' usquabae we'll face the deevil.'

After 12 years of violence and recrimination, peace came gradually to the district. The Act of 1823 had been followed by a vigorous campaign of suppression, and by 1836 most of the smugglers had returned to their farms and the womenfolk to their handicrafts, for in this curious war the men were engaged mainly in fighting the excise officers and in transporting their whisky to the South, thus leaving the malting of the barley and the distilling to their womenfolk, who by themselves and with their fierce dogs, were fully a match for the gaugers.

Although illicit distilling did not cease altogether, George Smith was now secure and, with iron resolution tempered by foresight, he began to improve and extend his property. When he took out his licence in 1824 the productive capacity of his Upper Drumin distillery was only 50 gallons a week. By 1839 he had raised it to 200 gallons, and still the demand for his whisky grew. In 1850 he added another smaller distillery at Delnabo, above Tomintoul, and called it 'The Cairngorm'. It was served by the Ailnack burn which in spate is black as soot, and George Smith, deciding rightly that quality must not be sacrificed to quantity, made up his mind to concentrate his whole production in the Glen which had brought him fame and wealth. In 1858 the Upper Drumin distillery was destroyed by fire, and, after removing some of the machinery including the original malt mill, George Smith obtained a fine piece of land from the Duke of Richmond and Gordon at Minmore and there built the distillery which, greatly extended and improved, still stands as the one and only Glenlivet Distillery. With its creation the Cairngorm Distillery was scrapped.

In the early days marketing his whisky was a serious problem for George Smith, for the inaccessibility which had favoured Glenlivet in the smugglers' war was a heavy handicap in peaceful conditions. There was no railway within practicable reach, and the whisky had to be carried in horse-carts over 35 miles of difficult country to the ports of Garmouth or Burghead on the Moray Firth and then sent South by boat. In 1863 the extension of the Speyside Railway to Ballindalloch brought some relief to a severe task.

Ballindalloch, however, is seven miles from the distillery, and even today horses are occasionally used in winter when severe frost and snow make the roads impassable for motor lorries.

As a farmer George Smith was, both by inclination and necessity, as great a pioneer as he was a distiller. For his distillery he needed to ensure supplies of barley of a quality on which he could rely. He was the first man to trench an acre of land in Avenside and in his own lifetime he reclaimed more than 300 acres of waste ground. As his whisky activities grew, he extended his purchases or feus of land, and with increase of wealth made cattle-breeding his hobby. Long before his death his Highlanders and crosses were winning prizes at numerous cattle shows. His heirs have carried on his tradition and have achieved great success as breeders of Aberdeen Angus and Shorthorns. Today there is still a fine herd of 'blacks' at Minmore.

George Smith died in 1871 at the age of 79. By then the 'bothy-still' and farm at Upper Drumin where he had started had grown into an estate of some 20,000 acres including 800 arable and 12,000 of hill-pasture. This growth in itself is a tribute to the achievement of a man whose reputation for straight dealing was as much the key to his success as his courage and foresight. The land that lies between the Findhorn and the Deveron has probably produced more pioneers and more self-made men per head of population than any other part of Britain. They include Cabinet Ministers in Ramsay Macdonald and Ian Macpherson, Dominion pioneers in the first Lord Strathcona and the first Lord Mount Stephen, publishers in Smith and Elder, explorers like Gordon Cumming and James Grant (the companion of Speke), famous journalists like James Gordon Bennet and Archibald Forbes, and a whole host of crofters' sons who emigrated to the New World and to Asia to build railways, run banks, and make fortunes for themselves. In this gallery of remarkable men George Smith, by his contribution to the land in which he lived, is entitled to a prominent place.

George Smith was succeeded by his younger son, John Gordon Smith, who had been a partner in the distillery for 20 years before his father's death. He, too, was a man of sturdy physique and great mental energy and during the 30 years of his reign he more than trebled the business. Quick to take advantage of every scientific invention, he installed new machinery, increased the number of bonded warehouses, and in 1896, when electricity was almost unknown in the Highlands, he set up a complete plant for the lighting of the distillery. In Banffshire he became a picturesque and popular figure, a pioneer of the Volunteer movement and a generous benefactor of the district.

His most important part in the history of whisky was the famous Glenlivet case. By 1850 Glenlivet whisky had already acquired a foremost name in the then comparatively restricted market for the product. Other distilleries, which sprang up later in Speyside, but not in the glen watered by

35

the Livet, sought to enhance the value of their own whisky by giving it the name of Glenlivet. Such was the wide abuse of the name that Glenlivet became known sarcastically as the longest glen in Scotland.

In 1880 John Gordon Smith, who had been trained as a lawyer and later received the honorary degree of Doctor of Law, took a test case. Had Glenlivet whisky to be made in the glen in order to justify the title of Glenlivet or could any distillery in the neighbourhood usurp the name? Mr Smith won a partial victory. The court decided that only the Glenlivet Distillery was entitled to label its whisky 'Glenlivet' without qualification. The other distillers, however, were not restrained from hyphenating Glenlivet with their own name. Many of them, as for example Craigellachie-Glenlivet and Benrinnes-Glenlivet, did, and continue to do so.

In 1901, John Gordon Smith died and was succeeded by his nephew, Colonel George Smith Grant of Auchorachan. The Grant connection was the result of a curious romance. During the period when George Smith, the original founder of Glenlivet, was in considerable danger from his former smuggling colleagues through his having taken out the first licence, a military guard was posted in the district. The young officer in command of it was a Grant. He fell in love with Margaret, George Smith's daughter, and married her. Their son, Colonel George Smith Grant, was apprenticed as a young man to his uncle, John Gordon Smith, and on the uncle's death succeeded him.

A tall and commanding man with a military presence, Colonel Smith Grant carried on faithfully the family tradition of distilling, farming, public work, private generosity, and, not least, volunteering. First as Colonel and later as vice-chairman of the Banffshire Territorial Force Association he did much to mould the character and temper of the 6th Gordon Highlanders which in the First World War was one of the battalions of the famous 51st Division.

Colonel Smith Grant died in 1911. His son, Captain William Smith Grant, was the owner until he died some years ago and the distillery was eventually taken over by Seagram's of Canada in 1979.

During the 171 years of its existence Glenlivet has grown from a small illicit still to a vast conglomeration of buildings capable of producing (in 1950) 7000 gallons of spirit a week and of storing 1,000,000 gallons of whisky in its 16 bonded warehouses, and 5000 quarters of barley in its granaries. While slumps and depressions have caused the closing, temporary or permanent, of other distilleries, Glenlivet has never stopped except under war restrictions. The same pattern of still as the founder, George Smith, installed at Upper Drumin is still used; the same method of steeping and drying malt is followed, and the heat and water come from the same sources. In spite, too, of the changes in taste and in manufacture which blending has introduced, Glenlivet remains, in the opinion of many connoisseurs, the premier whisky of the world.

Of its fame there is abundant proof, quite apart from the unbroken prosperity of the business. I have already quoted Hogg's eulogy of its merits. In *St. Ronan's Well* Scott makes Doctor Quackleben describe it as 'worth all the wines of France for flavour and more cordial to the system besides'. Later, the erudite George Saintsbury, as widely ranged in his ken of alcoholic beverages as in his knowledge of literature, gives his verdict that: 'Smith's "Glenlivet" knows no superior, if any equal, in its own country.' In his delightful paper on 'The Cellar of the Queen's Dolls' House' he fills the two quarter-casks of whisky which he allots to the dolls with Glenlivet and John Jameson.

How far Glenlivet justifies the high claim of the many who regard it as the premier malt whisky of Scotland, is a difficult and invidious task to decide. It established its name first; and quality has always been the first consideration of its producers. These are advantages which have helped its sale and its reputation. It is also true that, unlike most of the modern blends, its fame has been spread not so much by the spending of vast sums on publicity as by the free advertisement given to it all over the world by its habitual consumers.

There are, however, other excellent Highland whiskies, each of which has its own champions. Modern experts are cautious in singling out Glenlivet or any other malt whisky as the best. Greatly daring, Mr Aeneas Macdonald makes a list of 12 which he thinks will probably win universal acceptance. Glenlivet, of course, is among the select. The other whiskies listed are: Glen Grant, Highland Park, Glen Burgie, Cardow (Cardhu), Balmenach, Royal Brackla, Glenlossie, Longmorn, Macallan and Linkwood. He declines to fill the twelfth place, as he feels himself unable to decide between Talisker and Clynelish, each of which would be put first by its devotees.

Of these 13 distilleries Highland Park is in Orkney, Talisker in Skye and Clynelish in Sutherland. The remaining 10 are in the triangular kingdom of whisky of which Elgin is the capital and the Spey the largest river.

Mr Neil Gunn, who was an excise officer in the Highlands before he became one of Scotland's foremost and most Celtic authors, is more reluctant to commit himself and more catholic in his appreciation. He gives high praise to Glen Mhor, an Inverness whisky, and has a kindly word to say for Old Pulteney, a potent product from his native country of Caithness. He is an ardent champion of malt whiskies, and no other man has sung their praises with such lyrical enthusiasm.

'These generous whiskies,' he wrote, 'with their individual flavours, recall the world of hills and glens, of raging elements, of shelter, of divine ease. The perfect moment of their reception is after arduous bodily stress — or mental stress, if the body be sound. The essential oils that wind in the glass then uncurl their long fingers in lingering benediction and the noble works of creation are made manifest. At such a moment the basest man would bless his enemy.'

Only a Gael could have written this passage, and in it you have the essence of the Highlander's attitude to malt whisky. The choice is a matter of individual preference and palate, for, unlike many blends, malt whiskies have a marked individual flavour which has to be wooed and won by the palate, and when experts disagree, who am I to dictate my own prejudices?

I like Glenlivet because I am used to it. Obviously many other Scots have shared my preference. Hence the popularity of Glenlivet which in many countries is even today regarded as a synonym for Highland whisky. The greatest publicity it has ever received is William Aytoun's song, *Fhairson Swore a Feud*, which is known to every Scottish student:

Fhairson had a son
Who married Noah's daughter,
And nearly spoilt ta flood
By trinking up ta water.
This he would have done —
I at least believe it —
Had the mixture been
Only half Glenlivet.

The song has gone round the world, and Glenlivet has gone with it, although today, alas! it is hardly obtainable as a single whisky, for the vast bulk of its production has long been going to the blenders.

Another malt distillery which I must mention is Glenfiddich, partly because it is one of the few remaining independent malt distilleries in the Highlands, but mainly because it is in Dufftown, a little Banffshire town which I have known now for many years and which claims — I think with justice — to have more distilleries per head of population than any other town in the world.

Glenfiddich is not large, nor is it of ancient lineage, but I doubt if as much Highland grit and 'guts' were ever put into the building of any other distillery.

On the 19th of December, 1839, there was born in Dufftown to a Peninsular veteran, familiarly known as 'Old Waterloo', a son called William Grant. He went to the local parish school which 10 years previously had sent out into the world two remarkable men in the future Lord Mount Stephen and Field-Marshal Sir Donald Stewart. William Grant was good at his books, but, being poor, left school early to earn his living. Apprenticed as a boy to a shoemaker, he found the work uncongenial, and, eager for an opening, became manager of a lime works. With hopes of becoming a manufacturer of lime on his own account, he made a comprehensive study of the lime deposits in the

North of Scotland and, on one occasion, walked to Balmoral and back in two days, a distance of 120 miles, to find out for himself the prospects there. For want of capital his plans came to nothing, and in 1866 he entered the firm of Messrs Gordon & Cowie, then the owners of the Mortlach Distillery in Dufftown. Here he remained for 20 years and acquired a thorough knowledge of distilling and distillery construction. Like every Highlander of those days, he still longed to be on his own. His chance came when the plant of the old Cardow distillery came into the market. He bought it for £120.

Long before this purchase he had chosen the site of his distillery. Now he was to plan the construction and, with his sons and some outside help, to build his distillery with his own hands. The foundation stone was laid in 1886 and distilling began a year later.

For the first two years the distillery staff consisted of himself and of his sons who carried on their education at the same time.

When the Supervisor of Inland Revenue came to pay his first visit, he found Latin and mathematical textbooks lying all over the distillery. On asking to whom they belonged, he was told that they were the property of the stillman, the maltman and the tunroom man. All three were sons of the founder and, later, the stillman became Dr Alexander Grant, the maltman Dr George Grant, while the tunman, Charles Grant, became owner of Glendronach Distillery. Not unnaturally the astonished Supervisor reported that it was the most extraordinary distillery he had ever seen.

For once fortune bestowed its favours on the deserving. The enterprise flourished from the start, and four years later William Grant & Sons built Balvenie Distillery a little farther down the glen. Since then the firm has expanded until today it has its agencies in all parts of the world. Like its famous rival, Glen Grant, in Rothes, it has three great virtues. It has a remarkable record of individual enterprise. It is still a family concern. In its 'Special Glenfiddich' it still produces and bottles a pure malt whisky which sells mainly in the Highlands.

William Grant, who died in 1923 in his 84th year, came

of a remarkable family whose members, having come out for Prince Charlie in the '45, were scattered over Britain. His great-grandfather and his great-grand-uncle made their way to Lancashire, rose after many trials to be prosperous merchants, and eventually bought Sir Robert Peel's cotton mill. Noted for their good works, they are immortalised by Dickens as the Cheeryble brothers in *Nicholas Nickleby.*

William Grant of Glenfiddich inherited the family tradition of benevolence and charitable deeds and took the keenest interest in his native Dufftown, being an elder and precentor of the United Free Church, the leader of the town brass band, and an enthusiastic volunteer.

His portrait hangs in the luxurious London office of the firm and reveals a fine old warrior with moustache and mutton-chop whiskers and wearing the full Highland uniform of a major. Beneath the portrait is the following verse:

Lord grant guid luck tae a' the Grants,
Likewise eternal bliss,
For they should sit among the sa'nts
That make a dram like this.

There is no such luxury or ornamentation in the Glenfiddich office which is housed in a small stone building. It must be the humblest office of any distillery in Scotland. Yet it is sacrosanct, for the founder's hands helped to build the walls. They stand fast like the firm's Standfast whisky which today sells all over the world.

CHAPTER THREE

Balmenach

OH, WILLIE BREWED A PECK O' MAUT.

ALTHOUGH all malt distilleries, with their chimney stack, pagoda-like kilns and serried rows of warehouses, are much alike in their industrial ugliness, I must tell the story of Balmenach, the home of my Macgregor forebears and dear to my mother who was brought up there, and very dear to me through long association.

It stands on historic soil at the foot of the Cromdale Hills between two small 'toms' or hills about three-quarters of a mile from the ancient village of Cromdale. Tom Lea, where as boys and girls we played hide-and-seek on Sundays, far from the eagle eye of my Macgregor grandmother, was stripped bare by the lumberjacks during the last war and its pines now prop some coal-pit. On Tom Lethendry there still stands the ruin of an old castle where in 1690 the Jacobite refugees took shelter after the battle of the Haughs of Cromdale. Here General Buchan and his Highlanders, the remnants of Claverhouse's army, made the last stand for King James II and were routed by a mixed Anglo-Scottish force of King William III. The fight is commemorated in a celebrated Highland song which tells faithfully enough the course of the battle:

The English horse they were 50 rude,
They bathed their hoofs in Highland blood;
But our brave Clans, they boldly stood
Upon the haughs o' Cromdale.

Cromdale means 'crooked plain' and takes its name from the superbly beautiful stretch of the Spey which here winds its way in a semi-circular bend. On that fatal day of May 1st, 1690, it was certainly a crooked and red plain for the Jacobites, for King William's army, well primed with local knowledge and composed mainly of Scots, sprang a surprise by fording the Spey.

Less famous but almost as old as Glenlivet, Balmenach has a fascinating history. In the early years of the nineteenth century three Macgregor brothers left the smugglers' hotbed of Tomintoul and walked across the hills to Cromdale. One started a mill, the second took a farm at the Mains of Cromdale, and my great-grandfather James Macgregor settled at Balmenach. Doubtless, all three — and certainly James — had been engaged in illicit distilling in Tomintoul. Perhaps they had found the pace of smuggling too hot and considered Cromdale a quieter area for illegal operations. Be this as it may, James Macgregor combined the arduous task of hacking farms out of peat, bog and heather with the more lucrative sideline of illicit distilling.

Soon after the passing of the Act of 1823 he received a visit from the nearest excise officer. Their talk was friendly and began with a generous dram of pure malt whisky. When these preliminaries were finished to the satisfaction of both men, the excise officer mentioned shyly that he had his duty to perform and had better have a look round. Out went the two men to inspect the farm. All went well until they came to a rough stone building with a mill-wheel and a mill-lade by its side.

'What will that be?' asks the excise officer.

'Oh,' says my great-grandfather, 'that'll just be the peat-shed.'

Nothing more was said, and the two men went back to

the house for another dram and a talk about the crops and the prospects of the harvest. Then as the gauger took his leave, he said quietly:

'If I were you, Mr Macgreegor, I'd just take out a licence for yon peat-shed.'

My great-grandfather took the hint, and in 1824 James Macgregor shared with George Smith of Glenlivet, Mrs Gordon of Ballintomb, and the owner of Mortlach at Dufftown the doubtful distinction of owning one of the earliest licensed distilleries in the Highland kingdom of whisky. Since then the distillery has been entirely rebuilt, but some of the old buildings have been preserved. They include the original 'peat-shed' which today looks as if it really was what my great-grandfather called it.

Even in those days Balmenach whisky was well-known and was sold over what was then considered a fairly wide area. An entry in one of the old ledgers shows that on August 18th, 1824, William Milne of Aberdeen bought 10 gallons of Balmenach aqua vitae 11 over proof at 9s. a gallon. Other buyers in the same ledger include Sir Thomas Dick Lauder, Lord Selkirk and the Duke of Bedford.

The reader may well wonder why, at a time when whisky was almost unknown in England, the Duke of Bedford should have given an order for pure Balmenach. The answer was that he had married Georgina, daughter of the Duchess of Gordon, and was then living at Kinrara near Aviemore. The house has a history. The Duchess of Gordon retired there after a tragedy in her own life. One of the most beautiful women of her time, she was in love with an officer who was on active service. When he was reported killed, she accepted the Duke of Gordon under pressure of her parents. Soon after she was married, she learnt that the officer was alive and on his way home to marry her.

The shock and perhaps the suspicion that she had been deceived intentionally drove her to separate from her husband, and she retired to Kinrara, not to mourn for ever, but to kill her sorrows by an energy that never seemed to tire, whether she was entertaining her friends or canvassing recruits for the Gordon Highlanders whom she helped to raise. She inspired the same love of Kinrara in her daughter, the Duchess of Bedford, and both the Duchesses were buried in this neighbourhood; the Duchess of Gordon in the grounds of Kinrara and the Duchess of Bedford on the hillside overlooking the beautiful little Loch Gamhna.

In my great-grandfather's lifetime Balmenach prospered as a family concern. The Macgregors, however, are, or were a wild and lawless clan. Indeed, a cruel fate drove them to desperate deeds. In 1590 two Macgregors, finding themselves benighted, sought shelter and hospitality from a Colquhoun who had a house near Loch Lomond. The Colquhoun refused, and the two Macgregors retired, took a Colquhoun sheep, made their supper off it, and lay down to sleep. In the morning they were brought before the Colquhoun Laird of Luss who had them executed.

In revenge the Macgregors mustered their forces and, over 300 strong, marched towards Luss. In Glen Fruin they ran into a force of Colquhouns more than twice as large as their own. The battle was short and fierce and ended in a merciless slaughter of the Colquhouns. The fruits of victory brought no comfort to the Macgregors. Soon afterwards the widows of the slain Colquhouns appeared before James VI and I at Stirling, and, 'each bearing her husband's bloody shirt on a spear', demanded vengeance.

King James, who disliked the sight of blood, exacted the sternest punishment. The Macgregors were outlawed as a clan, forbidden to use their name, and deprived of their lands. Harassed now by all and sundry and, particularly by the Campbells, they withdrew into the mountains, and thus became in a literal sense, the People of the Mist, and lived mainly by plunder and rapine until their legal rights were restored in 1755. Inevitably they developed guile as well as grit, and their characteristics are perhaps best revealed by Rob Roy who, over-romanticised by Sir Walter Scott, tempered courage with canniness and a shrewd regard to his own private interests. In his famous novel Scott makes him say: 'Wise men buy and sell; fools are bought and sold.' It is a maxim which can be applied aptly in the whisky trade which has ruined more people than it has made.

The Macgregors, however, must have had more than their fair share of determination, for in circumstances, almost unparalleled in those savage times, they survived. My great-grandfather inherited the grit; and to 'guts' added vision, ability and an immense capacity for hard work. Towards the end of his life he was praised publicly by the Earl of Seafield as the man who had done most for Strathspey by making farms where none had previously existed.

James Macgregor married a Cumming or Comyn, as it was first spelt in English history, and brought up a family of 16. In 1850 John Macgregor, one of the younger sons and my grandfather, emigrated to New Zealand and, settling in the South Island, prospered as a farmer. According to New Zealand records, he discovered gold, but, preferring a farm in the bush to the uncertainty of gold under the ground, he did not follow up his claim.

After my great-grandfather's death, evil days fell on Balmenach. My Cumming great-grandmother was extravagant. With whisky — and strong whisky at that — always on the table or in a keg beside the dining-room door, the sons at home ran wild and died young, and in 1878 John Macgregor, who by this time had made a comfortable fortune in New Zealand, was summoned home to save the family. He answered the call, but after examining the financial position, removed his mother and her daughters to Burnside, half-a-mile farther up the Cromdale burn, and assumed full control on the sound capitalist principle of 'my money, my distillery'.

Within the first year of his ownership he narrowly escaped financial disaster. The same storm, which on the Sunday evening of December 28th, 1879, caused the Tay Bridge disaster, blew down the Balmenach chimney stack. The heavy stack fell through the roof of the stillhouse while the stills were at work and the hot spirit poured down into the furnaces starting a fire which threatened the complete destruction of the distillery. Fortunately, the stillman kept his head, opened the discharge cocks and ran the liquor into the sewers. The distillery therefore received only minor damage. It was a lucky escape, for the distillery was not insured, or at best very inadequately covered.

My grandfather died in 1888, and his widow, a remarkable woman, who, in the opinion of the leading Elgin lawyer, was 'worth all the distillers put together both in character and in business acumen', succeeded. Much against his will, my uncle Jim, who also had gone to New Zealand, was brought back to run the distillery. His unwillingness was to be justified, for by now bad times were coming for the whisky trade.

It was at this time that Balmenach, or a house in the neighbourhood, began to be my holiday home, and in the course of years I could hardly help acquiring a rudimentary knowledge of how malt whisky is made. I shall try to describe the process as simply as I can.

First comes the barley which must be well ripened, reasonably dry and, above all, capable of fermentation. The process of malting the barley is fascinating, for it involves man's successful interference with nature. Each grain or corn of barley consists of a tiny barley plant enclosed in a skin which itself is packed in an outer skin or skins containing starch. Nature has provided the tiny barley plant with this storehouse of starch in order to supply it with food during the early stages of its life. It is the task of the distiller to deprive the plant of its food and to convert the starch into fermentable sugar.

This malting process is performed by stimulating germination and then arresting it. The operation is a delicate one, for, if germination is allowed to proceed too far, much of the starch which the distiller requires for his malt would be consumed by the barley plant. To start with, the barley is placed in large low tanks called 'steeps'. Water is poured on it, and the barley is allowed to remain in the steep until moisture has penetrated every grain. Depending on the judgment of the maltman, this first part of the process takes from 40 to 60 hours. Then the barley is taken out and spread evenly over the floor of the long low-roofed malt-barns which are a feature of every Highland distillery. Here it begins to germinate, while men with large wooden shovels turn it over in order to maintain an even growth. In order to feed and satisfy the appetite of the growing plant, the grain, during germination, develops diastase, a compound which has the power of attacking moist starch and converting it into sugar. When restricted germination has reached this stage, the process is stopped, and the malt is then placed in the kiln, a chamber with a perforated mesh floor below which a peat fire is burning. The smoke passes up through the malt, dries it slowly and gives to it the peaty flavour which distinguishes most Highland whiskies.

The dried malt now goes to the mill where it is bruised but not ground fine. From the mill it goes to the mash tun. Here it is mixed with hot water at a carefully regulated temperature and stirred by machinery until the sugars in the malt are dissolved in the mash. The liquor thus obtained is then strained off and produces a sweet, still, non-alcoholic liquid which is known as the 'wort'. As a small boy I was often allowed to taste this sugary water and found it pleasant. It has long formed the basis of the various extracts of malt on which growing children are nurtured. Nothing, incidentally, is wasted in a distillery; the grains left over the 'wort' has been run off are used for cattle feed.

Now comes the stage of fermentation, and the brewer, a very important man in every distillery, takes charge. The 'wort' is passed into the fermenting vessels, huge round vats capable of holding anything from 2000 to 10,000 gallons of liquid. In whisky the fermenting agent is yeast which, when added to the liquid in the vat, 'attacks' the sugar and converts it into crude whisky. Other organisms such as bacteria play their part in giving a special flavour to the whisky, and some brewers are so fearful of any change affecting their product that they will not allow even a cobweb to be swept away from the vat room.

The process of fermentation lasts from two to three days by which time fully fermented liquid has been created. It contains crude whisky, yeast and various by-products, and also a quantity of unfermentable matter. The liquid thus produced has an alcoholic strength of only 10% or so and is now known as the 'wash'.

All is now ready for distillation, a process which for malt whisky requires the use of two stills. The 'wash' is conducted into a large vessel called the wash-charger which feeds the first of the two stills known as the 'wash-still' and the 'spirit-still'. The 'wash-still' is like a huge copper kettle with a long spout turned down and extended through the wall of the still-room to the 'worm'. This is a coiled copper pipe which lies in a large vessel of cold water. In the wash-still the 'wash' is heated to boiling point until the alcohol and other constituents of the malt rise in a vapour. This vapour then passes through the worm where it is cooled into liquid form.

This first distillate, known technically as 'low wines', is now ready for treatment in the 'spirit-still'. Here the same process of vaporisation occurs, but is much more complicated, for before distilling potable spirit from the spirit received, the stillman has to eliminate and distil into another receiver the raw first runs and the undesirable last runs called 'foreshots' and 'feints'. It is the most delicate operation in the making of whisky and demands great skill on the part of the stillman. He relies mainly on his experience and judgment, but has a further check in the hydrometers in the Distiller's Safe. This 'safe' is a brass case about the size of a large cabin trunk. Its sides are made of glass, and behind the glass are the hydrometers. The pure malt whisky from the spirit-still is passed into this safe, and here, through the glass, the stillman can test scientifically the strength and quality of his distillation. If he is satisfied with the result, he runs off the flow into the spirit receiver from which it is pumped to the storeroom and filled into casks.

The stillman, nearly always a splendid type of man with a sturdy belief in his own art and a scarcely concealed contempt for chemistry, now has the malt whisky which he wants. It is, however, not yet ready for drinking. Malt whisky, which emerges from the spirit-still as clear as gin, has to be matured in order to rid it of impurities and to improve its flavour. The choice of cask is therefore all-important, and the best is an oak sherry cask. It was, in fact, the sherry in the wood which gave the malt whisky its rich amber colour, and depending on the size of the cask, malt whisky is at its best between the ages of eight and 15 years.

Today sherry casks are not only expensive, but insufficient in supply for the requirements of the trade. The casks are often used twice, and a second filling produces a lighter colour, but the commonest substitute is an oak cask specially treated in order to give the same colouring as sherry. Nowadays, in order to obtain standardisation of colour the big whisky firms who control the trade use a solution of caramel.

The genius who first discovered that whisky improved in wood remains, I think, unknown. The use of the sherry cask and the consequent colouring of the whisky were probably accidental, and whatever the advertising wizards may say, the colouring in itself has only a small effect on the flavour. Glen Grant produces a clear, pale whisky and it is one of the best. Be this as it may, the use of the sherry cask was of great benefit to the trade in its conquest of the English market, for the richer class of Englishman who had to be wooed from brandy and soda would probably have spurned a pale whisky.

Malt whisky is run into the cask at 11.2 degrees over proof and with increasing years loses some of its strength. When the time for bottling comes, the whisky is reduced to the customary standard of 30 degrees under proof. Contrary to a widespread belief, whisky does not improve in the bottle.

One other technical detail which may interest the reader is the mystery of 'proof'.

It is entirely an arbitrary standard which today enables the Government to tax the strength at which it is to be sold, and the stillman the strength at which it is to be produced. In olden days proof was established by the primitive method of pouring a little spirit on a small patch of black gunpowder. If the spirit left the powder dry enough to ignite, it was over proof. If the powder remained a muddy mess, the spirit was under proof. Today the standard is accurately measured by a patent hydrometer. The formula for measuring 'proof' is slightly complicated and all the consumer need remember is that 'proof' spirit contains, as near as need matter, equal weights of pure alcohol and distilled water and that the greater the alcohol content the clearer looking the whisky.

Today, the strength of whisky is measured much more simply by the percentage of pure alcohol it contains. This now appears on all Scotch whisky bottles.

It remains to be said that, while most of the labour in a distillery can be called non-skilled, the key men, apart from the manager, are the stillman, the brewer, and the head maltman. The average number of men required to run a distillery varies between 20 and 30. Most of the men grow up and live with the distillery, and at Balmenach they were part of an isolated community in which everyone was cared for in sickness and in health.

Balmenach remained a family concern until 1897 when financial stress and heavy expenses in Malaya, where another Macgregor uncle, Alister, having failed in coffee, had started to grow rubber, compelled the Macgregors to turn it into a limited liability company, with a capital of £120,000 divided into 6000 Ordinary shares of £10 each and 6000 Preference shares of the same value. At the statutory meeting on April 27th, 1897, it was announced that the Preference shares had been applied for five times over. The Macgregor family kept all the Ordinary shares and thus retained the control. My uncle Jim, in his younger days a wonderful friend and companion to his nephews, became the first managing director.

With new money my uncle made many improvements. The one which gave the biggest thrill to my second brother, now headmaster of Sedbergh, and myself was the private railway from the distillery to the railway station at Cromdale. We made great friends with the engine driver, a magnificent figure of a man whom we called 'Long John', and very soon we were installed in his cab pretending that we were driving the engine.

As far as we could see, the conversion of the distillery into a company made no difference. Directors came occasionally to stay with my uncle, fished with him, took their dram and departed. We liked them, especially those who gave us tips, and we spent their gifts on fishing tackle. In other respects there seemed to be no change. The distillery remained our playground, and on wet days an empty malt barn made an ideal pitch for indoor cricket or tip-and-run. We were allowed to run free from a very early age. The Cromdale burn, then full of lusty trout, ran past the distillery. Higher up, it was fed by several tributaries, and, armed with shilling rods and a tin of worms, we wandered at will, roaming what seemed to us vast distances and flushing snipe from the bogs and grouse from the heather at almost every step. Then, with full baskets, we returned home, leg-weary but triumphant, to show our catch.

We were on good terms with everyone from Kenny, the shepherd who lived far up the burn-side, to the excise officers who had neat little houses close to the distillery warehouses.

Kenny excited both our admiration and our awe, for every year he used to walk his sheep the hundred miles and more to the sales at Perth, driving them slowly so as not to exhaust them, finding choice pasture for them, piloting them safely across rivers and burns in spate, and of course sleeping out with them in all weathers. A red Scot with beard and bronzed face, he had the legs of everyone in Strathspey. Once or twice a year, at the Cattle Show or on other special occasions, he let himself go and, with the whisky in him, backed his dogs against all comers. But for the most part he was a man of few words, tireless in his care of his sheep, and fearing no man. He was almost the last of his kind in Strathspey, and I can see him still striding across the hill, his cromach in his hand, and, like McAdam in *Owd Bob*, muttering great love-oaths to his dogs.

As for the excise officers, although I did not fully understand the nature of their functions, I shared in a mild manner the suspicions harboured of them by all the distillery men from the stillman to the youngest hand. The thirst of the Highlander is notorious and, although his standard of honesty is high, whisky does not come within its ambit. In the interests of a rapacious Government it is the arduous task of the excise officers to ensure that not a single drop of whisky escapes the payment of the official duty. Their control extends from the malt room to the bonded warehouse and is never relaxed. They know all the tricks of the distillery hands, and clever indeed is the man who can defeat their vigilance. The distiller's safe, where the final check of the spirit is made, is kept securely under lock and key, and the stillman has to do his job through glass.

In short, the gauger is like a zealous gamekeeper who is

always on the watch for poachers. For this reason excise officers maintain a certain reserve and go about their business
in a solemn and serious manner. Nevertheless, they are
scrupulously fair, nearly always tactful, and sometimes helpful. At Balmenach I found among them several friends who
had sweets in their pockets for a small boy and gave him tea
when he was late for his own.

When I was much older, I had good reason to be grateful to a Balmenach exciseman. After I had written *Memoirs
of a British Agent*, my income-tax affairs were in a muddle.
I neglected them and was summoned to a meeting by my
inspector. With some trepidation and a sense of guilt I
entered the room and was greeted solemnly by a stern-look-
ing man.

'We have met before', he said.

I looked at him but, unable to recognise him, could only
answer: 'Where and when?'

He replied: 'When you were a small boy and I was an
excise officer at Balmenach.' Instead of reading me the Riot
Act, he helped me to straighten out my affairs.

Several of the Highland excise officers have made distinguished careers and two or three have won fame in other
professions. I have already referred to Neil Gunn with
whom I once spent a very pleasant evening in Inverness, dis-
cussing Scottish nationalism and the new Celtic dawn and
drinking excellent whisky. Later still, I was to meet Maurice
Walsh who spent the best years of his life as an excise officer
in the Highlands. No-one has a better knowledge of the
Strathspey and Speyside distilleries. From the Highlands he
took his wife and the inspiration of his books which today
sell hundreds of thousands of copies both in Scotland and
in the United States. He was over 40 when he wrote his first
novel. It was an immediate success, and since then he has
never looked back. At least two of his novels deal with the
Tomintoul and Strathspey country, and one of my lasting
regrets is that I never met him on the various occasions
when years ago he visited Balmenach.

Small in stature with fine features, blue eyes, white hair
and a neatly pointed beard, he has all the charm of his race
and the graceful manners of a Spanish hidalgo. When

Ireland became a free state, he returned to his native land to help the Eire Government set up its own excise. Now 70, he has retired and lives near Dublin. He carries his honours with unassuming modesty, talks with the mellifluous ease of a Gael, and is a lovable and much loved figure. President of the Irish P.E.N., he comes back to the Highlands every year. He, too, is a connoisseur of malt whisky. Indeed, if anyone wishes to taste the best malt whisky that exists today, I would say to him: make friends with an experienced excise officer.

In addition to Lord Snowden who began his career as an excise officer in the Highlands, Scotland can claim another distinguished ex-gauger in Sir Arthur Tedder, the father of Marshal of the Royal Air Force Lord Tedder. We shall hear of Sir Arthur Tedder later on in connection with the Government's attempt to introduce prohibition during the First World War.

By 1905, when I first went abroad, Balmenach, although not one of the largest malt distilleries, had grown vastly since the days when my great-grandfather set up his illicit 'peat-shed'. No figures are available of the output in the early part of the nineteenth century, but I have in my possession a warehouse keeper's 'Receipt for Spirits Warehoused' for the week ending January 8th, 1862. It shows that for this period 206.4 gallons of spirit were produced from 110 bushels of malt.

Some idea of the growth of the distillery can be gained from a comparison with the output of the same week in 1950 when 6682.4 gallons were produced from 2480 bushels of malt. The reader will notice that the ratio of bushels of malt to gallons of whisky was far higher in 1862 than it is today. The reason is fairly obvious. Improved methods of distilling and a more careful selection of the barley have made possible a higher yield of whisky per bushel of malt.

On a rough calculation the annual output of Balmenach whisky in 1860 must have been approximately 7605 proof gallons. By 1880 it had reached 90,000 proof gallons. For 1950 a record output of over 259,000 gallons was achieved.

To this increase many men and many factors beyond the

control of Balmenach have contributed, but the chief credit belongs to my great-grandfather who, starting with nothing except his own wits, laid the foundation of this great enterprise and proved, as many Scots have proved, the truth of the Taoist saying: 'He who has little shall succeed.'

The obverse is: 'He who has much shall go astray', and both sayings can be justified by many examples from among the distillers to whom whisky is an ally to the strong and a subversive Fifth Column to the weak.

CHAPTER FOUR

Fine Folks

ALTHOUGH I'VE TRAVELLED FAR AND FAST,
I COUNT MYSELF FOR HIGHLAND — BLEST.
MAY CROMDALE BE MY HOME AT LAST
AND SPEY FLOW GENTLY WHERE I REST.

AT THE turn of the twentieth century life in Strathspey was very different from what it is today. Motor cars were so rare as to be virtually nonexistent, and the invasion of tourists on a, large scale had not begun. The land on both sides of the Spey was owned by two landowners, the Dowager Countess of Seafield and the genial Sixth Duke of Richmond and Gordon. Queen Victoria was still alive when I went to Fettes in 1900, and the widowed Countess of Seafield, who had endured many sorrows in her life, followed the Queen's example of austerity and seclusion. In a semi-feudal manner she kept a watchful eye on her estates and was by no means lacking in business acumen. A framed print of her portrait hung in the houses of all her tenants. Presumably it was a gift, for it portrayed her as a young and graceful woman. She visited the sick and gave bounty to the poor, but she was a remote figure more respected than liked by her people. As a boy I saw her occasionally when she drove out in her carriage, and, like everyone else in the neighbourhood, took off my cap as she passed. The salute was acknowledged by the slightest bend of the Victorian bonnet which she always wore. Her features seemed set in an eternal expression of sorrow, but her will was like steel, and no-one ever challenged it with impunity.

The Duke of Richmond and Gordon was more human and adopted a paternal attitude to his tenants with whom he was deservedly popular, for he never allowed his factors to press a poor farmer for the rent and he gave generously to local institutions and charities. But as great landowners both the Dowager Countess of Seafield and the Duke were 'fine folks' who scarcely entered into the lives of the people. Even more exclusive were the millionaires to whom they let their moors and deer-forests. To Tulchan, leased for many years by the Sassoons, came Edward, Prince of Wales, soon to become King Edward VII, and the Duke of York, the future King George V, to enjoy the grouse-shooting in a privacy which we shall never see again.

Among the people, on the other hand, everyone knew everyone else. Although money was scarce, hospitality was truly Highland. Fishing for trout, too, was more or less free, especially for boys, and many were the occasions when my brother and I, tired and wet to the skin, knocked at a cottage by the burn we had been fishing and were regaled with scones and oatcake, jam, 'crowdie', and tea or fresh milk. To have offered money, even if we had possessed any, would have been an insult.

Gaelic was still spoken by the older men and women, and on Sundays there were Gaelic services both in Cromdale and in Rothiemurchus. These services preceded the English service, and often we had to wait outside the church until their long sermon was over and the congregation trooped slowly out through the door; the older men, mostly bearded with long hairs protruding from their ears and dressed in black as solemn as their faces, and the women and children in their Sunday best.

Fine, hardy types they were; a little self-righteous perhaps, as the spirit of the times demanded, but God-fearing and full of the dignity that comes to men who live according to rule and who fight manfully an unequal battle with the unyielding soil. Away from church they could relax and tell wondrous stories of warlocks and kelpies and legendary heroes of the past. They knew every scrap of history of their own villages, for neither they nor their forebears had ever strayed far from them. They spent the long winter evenings in reading, and though their books were few, they knew them thoroughly, especially the Bible which they quoted readily to point a moral and illustrate the difference between right and wrong. Nor were they wholly ignorant of the outside world, for they received batches of letters from sons and brothers who had emigrated to the United States or to Canada, Australia and New Zealand. Stern parents, they were better educated than the urban or, for that matter, the Highland youth of today.

If they were servile at all, it was in the presence of the minister who, far more than the landowners, held sway over the community and, knowing that the fear of hell was strong in his congregation, sometimes exercised his power with undue severity. Often a great preacher, he was the master of his flock, the supreme arbiter in every family quarrel, and the terror of every ne'er-do-weel in his parish. If the reader wishes to realise the power of the Presbyterian Church in the old days, let him study Raeburn's superb picture of the Reverend Robert Walker, minister of the Canongate Kirk, skating on Duddingston Loch. The portrait is Raeburn's best and, long held in private hands, now hangs in the National Gallery in Edinburgh. One glance reveals not only the graceful movement of the skater but the supreme self-assurance of the man himself. It is the living portrait of one holding authority and fully confident of his ability to wield it. True, it was painted as long ago as 1784, but until the beginning of the present century the Highland minister retained the same consciousness of his privileged position and much of the same authority over his congregation. As a boy I rarely met a minister who did not inspire me with awe and with a feeling, doubtless amply justified, of guilt.

If religion and an inflexible faith in a future life were the spiritual virtues of those days, hard work and thrift brought one material reward. Whisky was then no luxury attainable only by the rich. It was the poor man's drink and the price was well within range of his modest purse. Prime malt Glenlivet and Balmenach whisky sold at half-a-crown a bottle, and everyone drank it, in the main with discretion and a fine appreciation of its flavour.

True, there were habitual drunkards: escapists from the hard way who could not pay their rent or had a scolding wife or who suffered merely from weakness of the flesh. They were seldom violent, nor did they drink at home, but two or three times a week went into the nearest town, filled themselves slowly 'fou' and, strapped to their seat by the publican, were driven home by their ponies. Even when they fell out, they seemed impervious to rain or snow or heat or winter frost. They were bred strong, outlived most of the ministers and bankers, and confirmed the truth of the old French proverb that there are more old drunkards than old doctors.

On special occasions, too, like lamb sales or Cattle Show Day, almost the whole community used to go what was known locally as 'on the batter'. Then nearly everyone from the doctors, the staid elders of the Kirk, and sometimes a minister, to the humblest farm hand or tinker imbibed freely. Tongues were loosed and stories swapped, and kinsman gave kinsman the news of a whole year with the detailed exactitude of men who, in those days of slow transport, lived far apart and saw one another rarely. Admittedly at the end of the day the trail home was often wobbly, but I do not think that much harm came from these meetings. They brought a scattered community together, gave it consciousness of its cohesion, and fostered good fellowship. They were, too, a reaction against puritanism and the drabness of daily life. I remember a Highland saying of those days: 'One whisky is all right, two is too much, and three is too few.' Two makes you want another and after three you can't stop.

Except on these special occasions the hard-working portion of the community — and it was the vast majority — was sober in mind and sober in practice. In my boyhood whisky hardly entered my thoughts, much less my mouth. When the cycling craze gripped me and we made long trips to Elgin and Dufftown, we could not help noticing the mass of distilleries which marred the landscape of Speyside, but I had little curiosity about the spirit they produced.

My Macgregor cousin, who was born at Balmenach and knew every stone of the distillery, was of a more inquisitive turn of mind. In the chamber in which the whisky is tested, there is a round covered receiver full of new over-proof whisky straight from the still. On the top of this vessel a so-called dip-rod is fixed. By inserting it the excise officers can gauge the quantity of spirit contained in the receiver. My cousin found that by attaching a small dry sponge to the rod she could fill the sponge. Carrying it tenderly to some secret place, she squeezed the contents into a tumbler. As the spirit from the receiver is about 20 over proof, I presume that she diluted it with water or wore an amethyst ring which in the thirteenth century was believed to preserve the wearer from intoxication. Fortunately, being several years older, I had already gone abroad. Otherwise my fall might have come sooner and more dangerously. I should add that my cousin enjoys the most robust health and is still a magnificent horsewoman.

She was not the only person in the Highlands to yield to this form of temptation. When I was a boy, the distillery men at Balmenach were 'drammed' three times a day. In my innocence I assumed that this gift of free whisky came from my uncle's generous heart and I wondered if I should be lucky enough to find an equally kind employer. I was of course mistaken. The free 'dramming' was instituted for one purpose only: to counteract a temptation which existed then, exists today, and is apparently irresistible.

In his attempts to defeat the keen eye of the 'gauger' and of the manager, the whisky pilferer employs the most ingenious methods and, if his thirst is limited, he can escape detection for a long time. One inventive genius devised a hollow tubular belt which fulfilled the double purpose of keeping his trousers up and of serving as a safe receptacle for stolen whisky. He managed to fill the belt daily for several weeks before he was detected. During the last war, too, troops stationed in a Highland distillery did not take long to discover the same methods that my cousin employed.

Usually the pilferer is a connoisseur who seeks merely to procure for himself better whisky than he can get out of a bottle. Today, however, malt whisky is so scarce and so prized that pilfering for sale is on the increase. 'Dramming' is probably the best preventive, but nowadays even 'dramming' has to be watched with vigilance. I know of one distillery where the men, on receiving their dram, used to retire to another room on the pretence of wanting to add a little water. Instead, they put the whisky in a small phial, took it home, and, waiting until they had a full bottle, sold it at a fancy price. The manager defeated this little scheme. When the men now come for their dram, he pours the water in first. Today 'dramming' is forbidden by the Excise authorities, but from what I have written above I imagine that, in the Highlands at least, the ban is more honoured in the breach than in the observance and that no tales are told outside the distillery.

In those early days, however, I drank the pure water of the hill burn and knew nothing of the temptations which it created when it left its course to enter the distillery. To my second brother and me Strathspey was a paradise and we counted the days until the Easter, and especially the summer, holidays came round. Because we were happy we thought in our selfish innocence that everyone else was as carefree as we were. Looking back on the past, I realise now how narrow and circumscribed by poverty was the life of the community. Farmers and crofters extracted a bare living from the unfriendly soil, and farmhands were wretchedly paid. There were no cinemas and no money to support them even if they had existed. Only in the summer were there any amusements: concerts where the visitors, aided by a little local talent, faltered through sentimental ballads, bazaars opened by a visiting celebrity, and of course Highland games in which, apart from a few local races, professionals provided the dancers and the strong men. On the part of the locals, the main object of this entertainment was to draw money from the visitors' pockets, and on the principle of 'who pays the piper calls the tune' it was the visitors who had such fun as existed.

The winters were grim, especially for the minister and the doctor who were often called out to comfort the dying or to bring a child into the world. Roads were poor, and some of the crofts were difficult of access. On a cold winter's night the doctor would climb into his dog-cart, drive to the nearest point, and then, tying his pony to a post, clamber up the hillside through snow or sleet to the cottage where the expectant mother awaited him. The only refreshment available — and it was gladly offered — was oatcake and whisky. It was small wonder that in some instances whisky became more than a necessity. There was, however, no dereliction of duty. Discipline was stern and, if hypocrisy covered sins which today leap more readily to the eye, plain living and high thinking bred a fine race which, because it was physically hardy, was not spiritually unhappy.

Today all is changed. The huge Richmond property has been taken over by the Government to cover death duties, and the Highlands have become a summer playground of the townsman.

The older men still sigh for the past, but in the younger generation motor buses, cinemas, and dance halls have created new desires, and for a long time now there has been a strong tendency among both the young men and the young women to leave the Highlands for the cities of the South. Two World Wars, which took a heavy toll of Highland blood, have unsettled them. It is not so much their thirst for amusement, speed and excitement which drives them forth as their unwillingness and, indeed, inability to live the old life of simple fare and hard work. Nevertheless, if limitation of desire is the secret of happiness and survival, and I believe that it is, I doubt very much whether the Highlander of today is as contented as were his forebears.

Fortunately, there is now throughout all Scotland a strong reaction against the persistent neglect of the Highlands. Schemes for hydroelectric works, re-afforestation and light industry are in various stages of development and, best of all, farming has been given a new stimulus. In recent years I have found some of the keenest farmers among the younger men who, in spite of, or perhaps because of, their war experiences, are determined to make their living out of their native soil.

In my boyhood beer was to be had in the hotel lounges of the larger Highland towns, but no Highlander regarded it as anything more than a substitute for water. Today the price of whisky is almost prohibitive to the men who make it, and all they can now afford is a whisky on Saturday night with a beer 'chaser'. The increase in the duty on whisky from 3s. 8d. per proof gallon in 1850 to £18 17s. 0d. per proof gallon in 1968 may have helped the Scottish breweries, but it has almost killed whisky as the Highlander's national drink. Now the price of a bottle is from 50s. to 59s. of which the Chancellor of the Exchequer takes into his maw 44s. as compared with 5d. per bottle in 1850. English beer, much of it now made in Scotland, has done what English arms never succeeded in doing. It has subdued and tamed the Scots.

In spite of Kipling's eulogy of the soothing and soporific qualities of beer and his denunciation of the inflammatory effects of whisky, I cannot believe that the change has benefited the Highlands. Each country has the drink which nature intended for it. Wine is the drink of the Mediterranean countries. Beer is the Englishman's tipple and is as much out of place in the Highlands as pollution in a clear-running trout stream. Vodka, akvavit, and whisky are the national drinks of Russia, Scandinavia and Scotland, and who will deny that Scotch whisky, as the only one which demands a connoisseur's palate, is the purest and noblest of the three?

If the opportunities are fewer, the Highlander has not lost his taste for whisky. When it is offered to him free, his thirst is unquenchable in its burning ardour. A Highland village, which I know well, made elaborate preparations to celebrate the Coronation of King George VI. A bonfire was built and, prompted by loyalty to his Sovereign, a local landowner presented a cask of whisky for the occasion. At the appropriate hour the bonfire was to be lit and the cask broached by a lady. Indeed, there may have been two ladies, for there were, I understand, two factions in the village. Perhaps for this reason, or perhaps because masculine hands were impatient to examine the contents of the cask, the fire was lit before either lady arrived. The logs and brushwood crackled. The whisky flowed, and very soon bonfire and villagers were on fire. By the time the ladies appeared, there was nothing left for them to broach.

On a minor scale similar scenes are sometimes witnessed at gillies' balls given by landowners or by shooting tenants, when even staid and sober head-keepers cannot resist the temptation of otherwise unattainable but surely not forgotten joys. On one occasion several sets of false teeth were picked up the next morning, and one pair was never claimed.

Taxation, in fact, has produced in the Highlands very much the same results as Prohibition in the United States. Denied by the high duty of what he has long been accustomed to, the Highlander of today tends to make up for lost time when a golden opportunity offers itself.

Today, too, the glory of Balmenach is gone. After the First World War the Macgregors, like many other small people, were hard hit. In 1922 the company was reconstructed under the chairmanship of Sir James Calder, and a few years later was sold to the already all-powerful Distillers Company Ltd. Today, its superb whisky goes to the blenders to be mixed with the combination of grain and malt which constitutes the whisky of the proprietary brands.

I paid my last visit to Balmenach in May 1950, and was shown over the distillery by Mr Scott, the manager, who, I was delighted to find, was not only a sturdy champion of the merits of Balmenach but had the history of the distillery firmly fixed in his memory and a high respect for its traditions. He showed us the old and the new, and I could see for myself the great improvements which had been made. When we had completed the long tour of the distillery, I wondered if he would give me a dram. I had been told beforehand that the days of drams had gone with the Macgregors. I was mistaken. After a little hesitation Mr Scott excused himself and left the room. Presently he came back with a bottle. The generous dram which he poured for me was a deep amber with a rich flavour that rose to my nostrils even before I lifted the glass. I drank it slowly like a liqueur and every drop sent a delicious tingle through my veins. The whisky was 15-year-old Balmenach and the strength was just about proof. It was, I felt, a last rite.

With a deep nostalgia in my heart I drove out alone to where the road ends at the very foot of the Cromdale Hills to take my leave of the landscape which I knew so well. It was a day such as one rarely experiences in these parts, for the sun shone from a cloudless sky, and in the heat the hills shimmered so that I could pick out every patch of heather and wiry grass to the very summit. I saw other patches which filled me with melancholy: standing stone walls bereft of their roofs, a strip of green sward or a group of rowan trees and silver birches originally planted to give wind-shelter to some Highland croft, but now mournful sentinels of a vanished home.

For 100 years farming and distilling had given the Macgregors a full life, had enabled them to rear large families, and send them out into the world, and to give work to a not unhappy community. Now all was gone. The little farms, which my great-grandfather had built out of moor and bog, had gone back to waste. The money had been dissipated and dispersed. The only Macgregor left in the district was the Macgregor of the mill, and he was in a bad way.

I saw again, as in a trance, the days of my childhood. Here until the age of 12 I had enjoyed the happiness of innocence. I had never seen death or thought of war. Europe and even England were utterly remote. It never entered my head that I should travel and, still less, that I should earn my living by my pen. The only author that I had met was Miss Marie Corelli when, as a visitor to Grantown, she opened a bazaar and I was introduced to her, shook hands with her shyly and fled. My world was Strathspey and Balmenach its capital, and how secure and how sufficing it was. Holidays in the Highlands seemed then all that was most permanent and desirable in life. Now the burn in which as a boy I had caught so many *enormous* half-pounders was a mere trickle.

As I turned back to my car, I took in the countryside in a broad sweep. It seemed more desolate than I had ever seen it before. The only sign of life came from the smoke of the distillery chimney, and the distillery belonged now, not to the crofter's sons who had built it, but to the rich industrialists of the towns. The change and decay that surrounded me and the fate of my own forebears were, I felt, typical of the Highland tragedy of the past 200 years. In the time of men still living, the population of the Highlands has diminished by a quarter.

Sad at heart, I raised my eyes to the hills, and my melancholy left me. If not everlasting, they at least would endure for my time and for the time of many generations to come. Hither I would return as I have always returned until I find my end in my beginning. It is, I feel, because the Gael is the greatest wanderer on the face of the earth that he clings so firmly to his past.

Before I end this chapter, I must mention another distillery which is an old landmark in my life. This is Dalwhinnie, which stands in the Drumochter Pass at the point where the waters begin to flow north, and is the highest distillery in Scotland. Dalwhinnie means meeting-place and is the real gateway to the Highlands. Through it Prince Charles Edward marched south to Prestonpans after raising his standard at Glenfinnan and through the distillery runs a portion of Wade's main road to the north. Here, too, was the battle ground where the Murrays of Atholl and the Macphersons of Cluny fought their frequent feuds. Close by is Loch Ericht dominated by Ben Alder where in Cluny's Cage Prince Charles Edward took refuge after Culloden, and in *Kidnapped* David Balfour lay sick while Alan Breck lost his money at cards. It was, too, at Dalwhinnie that the cattle-drovers and the whisky smugglers from the West and North used to meet and spend the night on their way to the markets of the South.

The distillery is comparatively modern and has had a chequered history. Started by three Highlanders in the whisky boom of the 1890s, it had already changed hands by 1905 when it was bought by an American syndicate which carried on the business until the end of the First World War. Then, after two more changes in ownership, it passed into the hands of the Scottish Malt Distillers Limited.

During the last war it provided a comic incident in my own life. In May, 1943, I spent a weary month in the local hotel recuperating after a troublesome illness. The rain fell daily, and, eager to get back to my war work, I wrote to Brendan Bracken, then Minister of Information, saying that I intended to return to duty at once and that I was ill with boredom. There was, I added, nothing in the place except a distillery, and it was shut.

Mr Bracken, determined that I should complete my cure, took immediate action, and the next night I was pulled out of bed to the telephone. A telegram marked Priority had arrived for me. Would I take it over the wire? The telegram ran: 'Remain till June 1st and open the distillery.'

For the next 24 hours the rumour ran through the district that a government expert had arrived to restart distilling!

CHAPTER FIVE

The Rise of Grain

*THE IMMORTAL SPIRIT GROWS
LIKE HARMONY IN MUSIC; THERE IS A DARK
INSCRUTABLE WORKMANSHIP THAT RECONCILES
DISCORDANT ELEMENTS, MAKES THEM CLING TOGETHER
IN ONE SOCIETY.*

IN THE preceding chapters I have given a largely personal account of the history and geography of malt whisky. I have explained that until well on into the second half of the nineteenth century malt whisky was mainly a Scottish drink, and that its manufacture from Scottish ingredients and by an unchanging and universally recognised process required two separate distillations. Whisky, in fact, was almost unknown in England when men still living today were born. In his book *A Roving Commission* Sir Winston Churchill writes: 'My father could never have drunk whisky except when shooting on a moor or in some very dull chilly place. He lived in the age of brandy and soda.' Of the 114 malt distilleries operating in Scotland in 1820 only five were catering for the English market, and all the five were Lowland distilleries. Ten years later an innovation in the process of manufacture led to the conquest of England and, eventually, of the English-speaking world. This was the invention of the patent-still.

The pioneer was Robert Stein, a member of a family famous for the beauty of its women and for the success of its main distillery at Kilbagie near Kincardine-on-Forth. One Miss Stein married John Haig who started Cameronbridge Distillery near Markinch, Fife; another married John Jameson who went to Dublin and founded the renowned Irish whiskey firm of John Jameson & Co. The Steins were the first regular exporters of Scotch whisky to London. They gained their permanent place in the history of distilling when in 1826 Robert Stein took out a patent for a still which produced alcohol in one continuous operation as opposed to the two distillations of the pot-still. Known as the patent-still it was superseded in 1830 by an improved still patented by Aeneas Coffey of the Dock Distillery, Dublin. With the introduction of the patent still came the manufacture of grain whisky and eventually the mixing of grain and malt whiskies into those blends which today are drunk by all the whisky-drinking world with the exception of the now, alas, decreasing number of Highlanders who remain faithful to straight malt.

The Coffey patent-still consists of two tall pillars called the analyser and the rectifier. Heated wort is passed down the analyser where it meets an upward current of steam. This process separates the alcohol from the wort, and the alcohol is then condensed on cool plates in the rectifier. As Mr Neil Gunn puts it in his *Whisky and Scotland,* 'a patent-still is an affair of two tall columns, heated by steam, into which wash is poured at one end and out of which practically pure alcohol pours at the other'.

The virtues of the patent-still are speed, relative cheapness and independence of geographical locality. For a licence-fee of £15 15s. anyone can build a malt distillery. He might take the best advice, choose a site close to one of the famous Highland malt distilleries, and yet lose his capital because his whisky might have the wrong flavour. For reasons which are not satisfactorily explained by the nature of soil and water and which so far defy chemical analysis, the characteristics of malt whiskies differ in the most baffling manner. Hence comes the well-known reluctance of successful malt whisky distillers to alter the slightest detail of the technique which they have always used. Patent-stills are free from this handicap. They produce no magic elixir, but they can be established anywhere without detriment to their product. In point of fact, all but one of the 13 grain distilleries of Scotland are Lowland and are situated in or near big towns with fuel and road and rail transport handy. As for speed, the reader will realise one material advantage of the patent-still when he is told that a large grain whisky distillery can produce as much whisky in a week as the average malt whisky distiller produces in his nine-month season.

Scotch grain whisky is made of unmalted cereals, preferably maize when it is obtainable, but rye and oats can also be used. A proportion of malted barley is also used in order to supply the diastase to convert the unmalted grain during the mashing process. Grain whisky is lighter in weight and less distinctive in taste than malt whisky. It does not improve in cask in the same manner or to anything like the same extent as malt whisky, but it is wrong to describe it as a neutral spirit. Costs of production were at one time much lower than for malt whisky. Today, the difference has been narrowed, but grain fillings are still about 35% cheaper than malt.

In one respect the patent-still has been of immense benefit to the nation, for from it comes the bulk of our industrial alcohol. In the early years of its existence a large portion of the raw product went to London to be made into gin or methylated spirits. A small balance, more or less raw and hot from the still, went to English publicans. In Scotland grain whisky found a ready market in the bigger towns of the Lowlands.

Although the blending of grain and malt whiskies, which is today a highly developed art, was not introduced until after 1860, Coffey's invention created a revolution in the whisky trade.

Patent-still distilleries sprang up almost in a night, but, as many of them soon disappeared, I conclude that their business cannot have been profitable.

But the Lowland Scot never lets go when he thinks that he has fixed his teeth in a good morsel, and by 1856 competition was keen enough to induce the leading patent-still distillers to enter into a 'trade arrangement', the object of which was to allocate the trade in fixed proportions. The six pioneers who accepted this arrangement were:

Menzies, Bernard and Craig	41.5%
John Bald & Co.	15%
John Haig & Co.	13.5%
McNab Brothers & Co.	11.5%
Robert Mowbray	10.5%
John Crabbie & Co.	8%

At the time of this arrangement the only stocks of spirit held by the six firms amounted to just under 17,000 proof gallons.

All the six firms were Lowland, and with the introduction of blending malt and grain whiskies, started first by the firm of Usher, the larger Scottish cities were to become the nerve centre of the trade. Perth, Aberdeen, Glasgow and Edinburgh had their share, but the metropolis was Leith.

The first Trade Arrangement lasted for nine years. Its progress, however, was unsatisfactory, and in 1865 a new Arrangement was concluded, the firm of Crabbie going out and being replaced by Macfarlane & Co. of Port Dundas, Glasgow. Mr John Haig became chairman of the new association which made various attempts to reach agreement on prices with the Irish and English grain distillers. They were so successful that in 1867 the price of Scottish grain spirit advanced from 1s. 7d. per proof gallon to the then record price of 2s. 7d.

The association, however, lacked cohesion and central control, and its career was marked more by apathy than by energy. Salvation came from an outside source when in 1875 Mr Robert Stewart of Kirkliston Distillery, West Lothian, and his accountant Mr Alexander Moore submitted a memorandum suggesting that the principal firms engaged in the distilling of grain spirit should form themselves into a limited liability company. The proposal was discussed at a meeting held in Castle Street, Edinburgh. The reception was favourable, but no decision was taken.

Less than six months later all internal difficulties were overcome, and on April 24th, 1877, the new company was formed and registered with a nominal capital of £2,000,000 divided into 40,000 shares of £50. Only 12,000 shares were issued and these were held by the six constituent firms who were:

M. Macfarlane & Co., Port Dundas Distillery, Glasgow
John Bald & Co., Carsebridge Distillery, Alloa
John Haig & Co., Cameronbridge Distillery, Fife
McNab Bros. & Co., Glenochil Distillery, Menstrie
Robert Mowbray, Cambus Distillery, near Alloa
Stewart & Co., Kirkliston Distillery, West Lothian.

In this manner there came into being the famous Distillers Company which in the space of 50 years was to assume virtual control of the Scottish whisky trade and to become one of the greatest dollar-earners in the British Empire.

The acquisition of other distilleries, which later became a distinctive feature of D.C.L. policy, began early. One of the first to be taken over was the Chapelizod Distillery in Dublin. At this time large quantities of Scottish spirits were sent to Ireland, because the total production of Irish grain whisky was then not more than 1,500,000 gallons annually. With characteristic optimism the Irish owners predicted a wonderful future for the new venture on the assumption that Irish whisky, which had already established itself on the London market, was better than Scotch and that the demand for it would be five times greater. The distillery was renamed Phoenix Park after the famous Dublin park where in 1882 Cavendish and Burke were stabbed to death. The title was an unhappy one, for the new distillery never realised expectations, partly because the quality of the product was not up to standard and partly owing to the waning demand for Irish whisky.

In the beginning, too, the D.C.L. had internal troubles, and the same suspicions and quarrels which had disturbed the harmony of the Trade Arrangement continued for some time to impede the smooth running of the new company. The distillers of those days were tough and independent men who had not yet learnt that compromise and unity are essential to the success of all amalgamations. In a speech, delivered not long after the registration of the company, Mr

W.S. Fraser, an Edinburgh lawyer, who knew the directors intimately, referred to 'the determined Haig, the politic Bald, the impetuous Macfarlane, the subtle Mowbray, the anxious Stewart, the cautious McNab and the bold Menzies'. It may be said that all these somewhat contradictory characteristics are to be found in the successful Scot, but in the D.C.L. they had to be welded before they yielded satisfactory results.

Whisky was now on the high road to England, and by 1880 the Dewar brothers, Alexander Walker, son of the original Johnnie, and a remarkable young Scot called James Buchanan were beginning to exploit the possibilities of the London market. The blending of grain and malt whiskies was developing rapidly, for the great firms which were coming into ascendancy were quick to realise that malt whisky gave the real character of Scotch to their product. It was and remains their contention that a blend of malt and grain is the ideal whisky.

Begun experimentally, blending has now become a highly technical process which depends for its success on a careful selection of the malt and grain whiskies to be mixed. Each individual blender has his own formula and his own methods. First, he collects the malt and grain whiskies of the age and quality corresponding to his formula. The proper proportions are then poured into a vat where they are mixed by compressed air. The content is run off into casks again and kept in the warehouse for a period varying from a month to a year. Some blenders prefer to blend their malt and their grain whiskies separately and to mix them only when they are ready for bottling. Once the finished blend is bottled, the product undergoes no change. If it is stored in wood, it continues to improve up to an age varying from 15 to 20 years. Today blended whisky has virtually ousted the single whisky from the market. Inevitably the qualities and the proportion of malt vary considerably in blended whisky, for although there are only approximately 100 distilleries in Scotland, the number of different blends runs to over 3000. It may be said, however, that the whisky of the better known blends is the product of many distilleries and that the great proprietary firms take every care to maintain the con-

tinuity of quality. Like the grain distilleries, the great blending centres are in the larger towns of the Lowlands.

Although many years were to elapse before blending
reached its present standard it was with this clear vision of
development that the Distillers Company embarked on its
course of acquiring control of both malt and grain distilleries. Its first three years of business had been fairly prosperous, and by 1880 the company, now eager to obtain a
Stock Exchange quotation, decided to offer a proportion of
its shares to the general public. To facilitate this operation
the nominal capital was reduced from £2,000,000 to
£1,000,000 made up of 100,000 shares at £10. Of these
100,000 shares the public was offered 43,334 fully paid-up
shares of £10 at £13 10s per share.

The response was amazingly poor. The offer was made
on June 16th, 1880, and by July 7th the public had applied
for only 6844 shares. It was not until March, 1883, that a
quotation was obtained on the Stock Exchange of
Edinburgh and Glasgow. Seven months later the shares had
soared to £23.

The London Stock Exchange proved to be a much harder nut to crack, and, owing to a technical flaw in the original issue of shares, the company had to overcome almost
insuperable difficulties before it could obtain a quotation.
The shares had to be registered and new certificates issued.
The public, not understanding these technical details, was
full of suspicion and raised many objections. The greatest
troublemaker, however, was a Mr Gundry, himself a member of the London Stock Exchange and an indefatigable let-
ter-writer who had made up his mind that his mission in life
was to resist the company's application.

Fighting a series of rearguard actions, he sorely harassed
Messrs Fraser, Stoddart and Ballingal, the company's law
agents. No explanation would satisfy him and, when the
lawyers sent him the fullest legal details of the revised
scheme, he wrote back saying that, if their letter was a sample of Scottish law, 'I thank God that I am not a Scotsman'.
The Scottish lawyers sent him the reply which he
deserved: 'Messrs Fraser, Stoddart and Ballingal acknowl-
edge receipt of Mr Gundry's letter ... and join with him in

thanking God that he is not a Scotsman.'

After nearly two years of legal wrangling the D.C.L. overcame the opposition. The first application for the quotation was made on January 16th, 1884. It was not granted by the Committee of the London Stock Exchange until October 27th, 1886.

Although well launched on its way to a career of continuous success, the D.C.L. was not yet wholly free from its birth pains. In the same year of 1886 the *Scottish News,* a Glasgow newspaper, made a violent attack on the company, prophesied a short life for it, denounced the management as incompetent, and asserted that several distilleries would shortly be closed and that the company's dividend would be reduced to 5%. The accusations, devoid of all foundation, were troublesome at the time. Ironically enough, they were ended by the sudden failure of the newspaper.

There was also opposition to the alleged monopoly of D.C.L. by the other grain distillers who were not in the amalgamation, and in 1888 a rival organisation was established by the creation of the North British Distillery Company with a productive capacity of two to three million gallons of spirit per annum. It did little more than ruffle the smooth course on which D.C.L. was now set.

A year later Mr William H. Ross, the real creator of D.C.L. and perhaps the greatest genius that the whisky trade has produced, joined the company as secretary and accountant. Thenceforth D.C.L. began in earnest a policy of expansion which, starting with the buying and building of both malt and grain distilleries and the development of new markets abroad, was to end in the acquisition of a vast multiplicity of interests connected with the numerous uses to which alcohol can be put.

Soon after Mr Ross's arrival the company began to experiment with the manufacture of yeast for bread. For a long time it sought to improve on an existing Austrian patent, and, as usual, the initial difficulties caused vexatious delays which were prolonged by the necessity of ensuring that the process conformed with the regulations of the Excise. By 1899, however, a separate subsidiary company, known as the United Yeast Co., Ltd., was formed to handle and to find a market for the output. We shall see later how valuable this development was to be to the British people in both the World Wars.

From its first days the company had done a small business in blended whisky for export. In the 1880s this side of the business began to expand with remarkable rapidity. World tours by the energetic directors spread the fame of whisky, and their campaign was sustained by effective advertising. For better or worse, blended Scotch whisky was not only conquering the English market but finding its way into the United States and the Dominions of the British Empire in ever-increasing quantities.

For more than a decade nearly all Scottish distillers reaped handsome benefits from the boom conditions. Then in 1898 came the inevitable slump. The fundamental cause was the innate passion of the Scot for gambling. The general assumption that the Scot is afraid to take risks in business is erroneous. No other race is more daring in speculation, and Scottish history is rich in examples of the disasters which overtook those get-rich-quick Scots who did not season speculation with caution. To give only one instance, the creator of the tragic Mississippi scheme, which brought ruin to thousands of Scottish families, was John Law, a Scot of great ability who founded the Bank of France. He was a wizard with figures, but his genius was wayward, and even the French bore him no gratitude at the time, as the following epitaph shows:

Ci-gît cet écossais célèbre,
Ce calculateur sans égal,
Qui par les règles de l'algèbre
A mis la France a l'hôpital.

A similar recklessness provoked the crash of the whisky 'boom' in 1898. The immediate cause was the so-called Pattison failure. In the early eighties of the last century a firm of blenders set up in business in Leith under the name of Pattison, Elder and Co. By methods which lacked both prudence and foresight they acquired a large share of the whisky trade and soon established themselves as a limited

76

liability company. The name Elder was dropped, and the title Pattisons Ltd. adopted. In point of fact the business was controlled by two brothers, Robert and Walter Pattison. Initial success went to their heads. They built themselves palatial premises in Leith and ran their business on a scale of splendour that was rare in the Scotland of those days. The wise men of the D.C.L. knew that the management was extravagant. The firm, however, sailed along gaily on the tide of the ample credits which the Scottish banks provided with surprising ease, and the unsuspecting public assumed that magnificence harboured success. Investors and speculators were drawn into the vortex of gambling. Under the stimulus of boom conditions the distillers doubled or trebled their output. New distilleries sprang up like mushrooms, and the shares were taken recklessly by the greedy public. Inevitably production soon exceeded the demand.

Then one day the rumour spread that Pattisons were in difficulties. It ran like wildfire through the country, and the bottom fell out of the whisky market. After vain and frenzied attempts to reorganise its affairs the firm suspended payment on December 6th, 1898.

The failure had a disastrous effect on the whole trade. Its more sordid aspect was exposed when the Pattison brothers appeared before the Criminal Court. The elder brother, Robert, who was the more responsible partner, was sentenced to 18 months' imprisonment. Walter was given eight months.

Scotland is a small country in which kinship and friendships are widespread. Although I was only 11 at the time, I remember vividly the shock of the failure. Next door to us lived a family in which there were two boys of more or less my own age. The mother was a Pattison. The family was hard hit by the failure. It was the first time in my life that misfortune had overtaken people whom I knew and liked, and this tragedy on the doorstep affected me poignantly.

Although the casualties among smaller distilleries were heavy, the strong and solid D.C.L. weathered the storm with comparative ease. Indeed, the failure was to facilitate the D.C.L.'s policy of amalgamation. It also gave them an immediate benefit in the acquisition of new property at a very low price. After the collapse of the Pattisons their assets were placed for realisation in the hands of the official liquidator, and the magnificent Pattison warehouses at Leith were put up for auction. They had cost the Pattisons £60,000. The D.C.L. bought them for £25,000.

The directors of the D.C.L., however, were fully aware of the dangers of overproduction and, although blending and export were carried on with full vigour, bought more distilleries in order to keep output within reasonable limits. They closed several distilleries temporarily, but retained the warehouses for storing purposes. These new acquisitions, cheaply bought in a low market, received an unexpected value when in 1903 Port Dundas, one of the largest distilleries controlled by D.C.L., was destroyed by fire.

CHAPTER SIX

The 'What is Whisky?' Case

BUT YOU'VE NO IDEA WHAT A DIFFERENCE IT MAKS,
MIXING IT WITH OTHER THINGS.

IT MUST not be supposed that the stupendous success achieved by grain whisky was pleasing to the Highland malt distillers. On the contrary, they were up in arms against this new and dangerous rival and objected strongly to grain whisky being sold as Scotch. More than once they had tried to induce Parliament to ban 'the trash' and, although they had failed, they were by no means prepared to admit defeat.

It was from London of all places that the first serious trouble came to the confident and by now highly prosperous grain distillers. It arrived suddenly and unexpectedly when in 1905 the Islington Borough Council took out summonses against a number of local publicans and off-licence holders for selling 'an article not of the nature and substance demanded'. The 'article' was of course grain whisky, and the summonses were serious, because if the court decided against the publicans and off-licence holders, the whole future of grain whisky would be jeopardised. Some of the men summoned were members of the Off-

79

Licences Association and appealed to the trade to support them.

It was an issue which could not fail to interest the D.C.L., and without wasting time the directors met and decided to fight the case. Simultaneously they prepared a pamphlet not only defending the merits of grain whisky, but also attacking the alleged impurities of malt whisky, and circulated it to members of Parliament.

The action, known as the 'What is Whisky' case, was heard before Mr Fordham, the magistrate of the North London Police Court, and judgment was given against the defendants who, on the advice and with the support of the grain distillers, decided to appeal. The only possible Court was Quarter Sessions, and it was not suitable for such a technical inquiry. On Monday, May 28th, 1906, the Court met at Clerkenwell under the chairmanship of Mr W.R. McConnell, K.C., assisted by a bench of lay magistrates. It held seven sittings and then gave no decision, because the bench was divided. Here was a deadlock which apparently could not be broken, and the malt distillers were jubilant.

In face of this serious situation the grain distillers and the blending trade met and decided that the D.C.L. should approach the President of the Board of Trade and request him to appoint a Committee or a Royal Commission to settle the whole problem once and for all. Progress, however, was slow. The President of the Board of Trade was Mr John Burns, the first working man to be a Cabinet Minister. Before joining the Liberal Government of the time he had been a Socialist. Apart from an early antipathy to capitalism, he had seen something of the evil effects of drink in big cities, and on his first visit to Chicago he had shocked the local Press by comparing the city to hell. Urged by the journalists to give himself more time to see the city before condemning it, he requested them to come back in three days. When they returned and asked him what his views now were, he lifted his hat and said solemnly: 'I apologise to hell.' He was not therefore likely to be a warm supporter of any branch of the whisky trade. And so it proved, for after several interviews with the trade delegates he refused to budge.

Help, however, came to the grain distillers from an unexpected quarter. The Islington Borough Council was as eager as the D.C.L. to have the matter settled and suggested a joint approach to the President. Faced now with a decision which he could not easily avoid, Mr Burns bestirred himself and in July, 1907, obtained the consent of Parliament to the appointment of a Royal Commission.

The D.C.L. girded itself resolutely for the fight. It prepared and inserted in the *Daily Mail* an advertisement announcing that D.C.L. was putting on the market pure Cambus whisky in bottles. This was a direct challenge to the Government and the malt distillers, for Cambus was a pure grain whisky unrelieved by any blending of malt. The object of the advertisement was to show to the public that pure grain whisky was pleasant and palatable. It was also lighter than pure malt whisky, and better suited to the weaker stomachs of the sedentary urban population. The best Scotch whisky was therefore a matter of the judicious blending of grain and malt. The advertisement was kept in the *Daily Mail* until the Royal Commission had concluded its findings. Then it was quietly withdrawn.

The Commission was formed on February 17th, 1908, with Lord James of Hereford as chairman. He was supported by Mr Laurence Guillemard, afterwards Sir Laurence Guillemard, Governor of Singapore, and six scientific and medical experts. The Commission's terms of reference can be summarised as follows:

To consider whether, in the general interest of the consumers, or in the interest of the public health it is desirable

1. to place restrictions upon the materials or processes which may be used in the manufacture and preparation in the United Kingdom of Scotch and Irish whisky or of any spirit to which the term whisky may be applied;

2. to require a declaration of the age of whisky and of the materials and processes used in its manufacture and to fix a minimum period during which any such spirit should be matured in bond.

Both parties to the dispute prepared their arguments with elaborate care. The case of the malt distillers — and it was a strong one — rested on the claim, supported by centuries of tradition, that 'Scotch Whisky' was clearly definable as a spirit made from malted home-grown barley, distilled by a special process, and matured to a recognised flavour and quality. It had therefore a special character which, because it could not be imitated, was of great benefit and value to Scotland. True it is that by this time home-grown barley had been partly replaced by foreign, but neither the manner of making Scotch whisky nor the local conditions which contributed to its quality had changed. Scotch whisky had a special flavour as easily recognisable as cognac or vintage burgundy. The defensive tactics of the malt distillers were based on taste and tradition. The whole romance of whisky, too, was on their side.

The malt distillers also waged a fierce offensive against grain spirit. It was, they asserted, a tasteless distillate which could be made from almost any material from grain and garbage to roots and rags. It was a neutral which was incapable of improvement by maturing. The malt distillers called it a 'silent' spirit unfit to rank with the 'loud' malt spirits which 'go down singing hymns'. To add a percentage of malt whisky to this silent and raw alcohol, colour it with a chemical, and to call the result Scotch whisky was a fraudulent deception which could be imitated in many parts of the world and would deprive Scotland of its exclusive right to the special character of whisky. The malt distillers also claimed that patent-still whisky was injurious to the health of those who drank it.

In refutation of these contentions the grain distillers brought forward formidable arguments both of defence and attack. They denied that blended whisky, as made in Scotland, was incapable of being improved by age. Blended whisky was made of a scientific mixture of grain and malt whisky. The best blends were mixed in proportions of roughly 50% malt whisky and 50% grain whisky and their flavour, the grain distillers argued, improved in wood.

They also claimed that blended whisky was purer than malt which contained fusel oil and other 'impurities'. They adduced medical evidence to support their assertion that blended whisky was less injurious to health than malt. Their case therefore rested on the claim that a scientific blending of grain and malt produced the best and the safest whisky. The Royal Commission issued its final report on July 28th, 1909. It was a triumph for the grain distillers and, in particular, for the D.C.L. who organised the whole defence and paid all the costs. By defining whisky as 'a spirit obtained by distillation from a mash of cereal grain, saccharified by the diastase of malt', the Commission made no distinction between pot still and patent-still or between Scotch and Irish whisky nor did it accept the malt distillers' contention that Scotch whisky was and always had been a distillate of wort made from malted barley.

The members of the Commission gave further satisfaction to the grain distillers by stating that they found no evidence to indicate that the form of still bore any relation to the wholesomeness of the spirit which it produced. Declaring that 'the trade in whisky seems to be honestly and fairly conducted', they ruled that no special legislation was required.

Their only other finding of any importance was in reference to compulsory bonding. Here again members of the Commission came down on the side of the grain distillers. After pointing out that pot-still whisky required a very much longer period of maturing, they decided that it was undesirable to fix a statutory minimum period for bonding.

The decision, made by a Commission described by Saintsbury as 'perhaps the most futile on record' and composed mainly of Sassenachs who knew little or nothing of the special merits of whisky, was a serious blow for the malt distillers who were bitterly resentful. Expression was given to their indignation by the Duke of Richmond and Gordon, a grandson of the Duke who, on behalf of Highland whisky, had been mainly responsible for the Act of 1823 which legalised distilling in the Highlands. Speaking at Glenlivet soon after the Royal Commission's decision, the Duke declared amid loud applause: 'Quite recently a public inquiry has taken upon itself to decide what is whisky. And I regret to say that apparently anything that is made in Scotland, whatever its combination, is to be called Scotch whisky. For my part, I prefer, and I think that most of those whom I am addressing now would prefer, to trust to their own palates rather than to the dogma of chemists, and to be satisfied with the whisky that is produced in Glenlivet as against any other quality that is produced in Scotland.'

For Glenlivet itself there was a special irony in the Royal Commission's decision in favour of the blenders. The pioneers of blending were the well-known firm of Messrs Andrew Usher & Co. of Edinburgh. Since 1840 they had been agents of Glenlivet, first for the South of Scotland and for England, and from 1864 for the whole world.

As a Scot of mixed parentage whose heart is Highland and whose head has at any rate a portion of Lowland caution and energy, I find it hard to decide whether the Commission's decision affected adversely the prestige and renown of Scotch whisky. At the time the malt distillers maintained that it did. Even today the fire of their wrath still smoulders and occasionally breaks out into flames, and the diminishing band of real connoisseurs continue to swear by the virtues of malt whisky and to drink it.

What is clear beyond doubt is that at the inquiry the grain distillers had the big money and the better brains. Moreover, they were astute enough to realise the advertising value of the title 'Scotch' and up to now have done a successful best to exploit it. On the other hand, by sanctioning grain alcohol as a permissible element of Scotch whisky, the Commission virtually gave supreme power to the blenders who now control all but a tiny minority of the malt distilleries. In its ultimate effect, the Commission's decision altered the taste of whisky throughout the world to the detriment of the connoisseurs of cultivated palate who drink for flavour rather than for frolic, and in favour of those millions, including many Scots, whose taste for whisky is largely determined by a desire for a stimulant or a spree. With perhaps too little knowledge of what it was doing, the Commission also opened the way for foreign competition, the effects of which in the United States and in the British Commonwealth may one day prove serious.

On top of these findings the whole whisky trade received an unexpected shock for which the Royal Commission was indirectly responsible. While it was sitting, Mr Lloyd George was preparing his 1909 Budget. When it was announced, he sprang an unpleasant surprise on the trade by increasing the duty on spirits from 11s. per proof gallon to 14s. 9d. and by changing the original licence duty of £10 for working a distillery to a tax on the actual amount of whisky produced. Taken off its guard, the whole trade complained. Mr Lloyd George consented to receive a deputation but, largely owing to the quarrel between the grain distillers and the malt distillers, he had no difficulty in getting his own way.

To the D.C.L. the findings of the Commission were a stimulus to further acquisitions and amalgamations. Freed now from all anxiety, the company prospered, and the period from 1909 until the outbreak of the First World War was rich in the development not only of blended whisky but also of gin and alcohol. By the purchase of patent-still distilleries in London, Liverpool, and Ireland, the D.C.L. not only assured for itself a larger share of the English trade in gin and industrial alcohol, but also removed the previous difficulty in coming to an arrangement with the English distillers regarding the control and sale of spirits for methylating. By forming the Industrial Spirit Supply Co. Ltd., with registered offices in London, the D.C.L. was soon in a position to control sales and, by avoiding the worst forms of competition, to sell its products to the public at a reasonable and steady price.

Two years before the 1914 War the whisky trade had recovered from the slump of overproduction caused by the Pattison failure and, although at the annual shareholders' meeting of the D.C.L. in July of 1912 the chairman again issued a warning against the dangers of overproduction, the main credit for the recovery must be given to the company. It can be said without dispute that hitherto the whisky trade, like the New York Stock Exchange, had been subject to a highly nervous condition in which booms and depressions alternated with disturbing rapidity. The D.C.L.'s policy of amalgamation gradually eliminated these undesirable symptoms. This was, and is still, its most valuable contribution to the whisky trade and the justification of its own existence.

PART II

The Whisky Barons

WE ARE NOT BANANA-EATING BOYS

MALAY PROVERB
(ANGLICE, WE WERE NOT BORN YESTERDAY)

CHAPTER SEVEN

The Dewars

IT CAME LIKE MAGIC IN A PINT BOTTLE.

IN SPITE of its initial successes the Distillers Company was still a comparatively small organisation, and many years were to elapse before it acquired anything like the supreme control which it holds today. In that golden age of whisky from 1880 to the First World War there were other great whisky firms outside the amalgamation. Their success had been no less astonishing than that of the D.C.L. Among these firms was the House of Dewar. The story of its rise from humble beginnings to its present magnificence exemplifies the cardinal virtues of the poor Scot of those days: grit, courage, thrift, plain living, vision, honesty, an immense capacity for hard work and the ability to grasp the golden opportunity when it presented itself.

In the year 1806 there was born to crofter parents one, John Dewar, in the little farm of Shenavil in the parish of Dull, about two miles from Aberfeldy. Brought up on simple fare, he was educated at the parish school four miles away. Summer and winter he made the journey there and back on foot. In cold weather he had to carry, in addition to his books, a goodly sized divot of peat to keep the school fire burning.

The croft was too small to support the sons, and John was originally destined to be a joiner. His elder brother James was already established in a joinery in Aberfeldy and, after serving his apprenticeship, John was taken into his brother's business. He was then 20. Two years later the postman of opportunity knocked at his door. A distant cousin, James Macdonald, had a wine merchant's business in Perth and wanted a reliable man to look after his cellars. He offered the job to John Dewar who promptly accepted it.

James Macdonald's premises were in the very heart of historic Perth. Close by was the site of the ancient Blackfriars Monastery where James I, the poet King of Scotland, was assassinated. A few steps further away was the house where dwelt the Fair Maid of Perth. The romance of the ancient city fired the heart of John Dewar. Well-content to make Perth his home, he married and settled there for good.

Assiduous in his attention to business and always doing more than he was called on to do, he was made a partner in 1837, and the firm was renamed Macdonald and Dewar. Nine years later he decided that he could do better on his own and, dissolving his partnership with his cousin, set up as a wine and spirit merchant in a small shop in the High Street.

The venture was not without risks. The times were marked by insecurity and confusion. England was in the throes of the conflict of the Corn Laws. In Ireland the potato famine of the 'Hungry Forties' was raging. Scotland herself was torn by the bitter controversy of the 'Disruption' of the Kirk. In spite of these disturbing conditions, a group of remarkable men, citizens of Perth, found, during the second half of the century, full scope for their vision and enterprise and succeeded in establishing not only the House of Dewar but also the greatest dye-works and the largest accident insurance company in Britain.

In 1846 whisky smuggling and illicit distilling had not yet ceased. No-one had yet dreamed of putting up proprietary brands of whisky in bottles. Here was an opportunity for John Dewar, and he was quick to seize it. For the first decade or more his trade connections were limited to the Perth area, but in 1860 he engaged his first traveller and began to push his trade both North and South.

In 1879, an important date in the fortunes of the firm, he took his son, John Alexander, into partnership. A year later the father died at the age of 74. His portrait shows him as a patriarchal figure with a high forehead, firm mouth, eyes well set yet withal kindly, and a magnificent white beard typical of the Scottish elders of that era. He had left to his heirs a business which, though not large, had been built on sound foundations and had safely weathered all the storms of the times including the failure of the City of Glasgow Bank in the '1870s', which sent an icy blast over a large area of Scottish industry.

John Dewar had done more than create a sound business. He had produced two remarkable sons whom he had brought up, as much by example as by precept, with the same discipline and same virtues of honesty and grit which had always characterised his own conduct.

When his father died, John Alexander Dewar was 24. Four years later he was joined by his younger brother, Thomas Robert Dewar, then only 21. Both men had been trained for the whisky trade and had served their apprenticeship in Leith which was still the whisky capital of Scotland. Both had received a sound education at Perth Academy, sturdy foster-mother of many famous men including William Archer, the dramatic critic, James Crichton (the 'Admirable Crichton'), Lord George Murray (the General of the '45), the Rev. James Watson (Ian Maclaren), and a host of scholars, divines and missionaries.

With the same sound judgment that their father had shown, but with more ambition and imagination, the two young men resolved to conquer the English market, and with this end in view John Alexander sent his brother Tommy to London in 1885. It was a big gamble. Scotch whisky was still little known across the Border, and to the Dewars themselves London was uncharted territory. Tommy Dewar arrived in the city with two letters of introduction. When he went to present them, he found one addressee dead and the other bankrupt. Before he could open his premises in 6 Warwick Street, Pall Mall, he had to find security for the rent.

Tommy Dewar was a born salesman, witty, dapper, genial and endowed with volcanic energy. The first task he set himself was to make himself known, and the Brewers' Show at the Agricultural Hall gave him his opportunity. On a short visit to London in the previous year he had noticed that musical boxes were much in evidence at the Show. Obviously music was permitted, and when the Show opened the next year the stentorian blast of a bagpipe deafened the Hall. The chairman was speechless with rage. The Committee rushed to Dewar and ordered him to stop, but the Scot threw out his chest and, asserting loudly that pipes were better than barrel organs and musical boxes, blew his brawest. The journalists swarmed round him. The Committee threatened legal action, but T. R. Dewar, knowing well that any publicity was better than none, continued to defy authority until he had finished his warbling.

After this performance all London knew him, and orders soon followed. Bottled whisky was in demand in hotels and restaurants, and in 1888, in the face of strong competition, Tommy won his first major success when he persuaded Spiers and Pond to take Dewar's as the sole whisky for all their establishments. Within 10 years of the founder's death the English market had been conquered, and the House of Dewar, now registered under the Trade Marks Act, was firmly established on the map of England. In 1894 the firm opened its first provincial branch in Bristol.

To meet the new demands and to ensure its own supplies of whisky, the firm began to acquire distilleries. In 1890 Dewar's obtained on long lease from the Duke of Atholl the distillery of Tullymet near Ballinluig, Perthshire, and six years later the brothers built their own distillery at Aberfeldy only a few miles away from the croft of their grandfather.

Within 10 years the business of John Dewar & Sons had grown so rapidly that it had vastly exceeded its financial resources. The two brothers, however, had character as well as ability, virtues which appealed to the Scottish bankers of those days more than large cash balances. Credits were therefore readily forthcoming. Although the brothers were not afraid of risks — indeed, at one period their bank overdraft amounted to £300,000, the bankers reaped a handsome profit from their sound judgment in backing the two Dewars.

So great had been the expansion of business that in 1894 the firm was turned into a private limited liability company with a capital of £100,000 and £50,000 debentures. The finance was not sufficient for the soaring business, and three years later the capital was raised to £600,000 divided into 35,000 ordinary shares of £10 each and 25,000 preference shares of the same denomination. The preference shares were offered to the general public at a premium of £1 and were largely oversubscribed.

Not content with the success which they had already won, the brothers looked for new fields to conquer. The whole world was now their target, and in 1892 Tommy Dewar set out on a two-years' tour which took him to 26 countries. Everywhere he went he appointed first-class agents, and soon after his return large orders for cases of bottled whisky began to pour in from all parts of the globe. Thanks to his salesmanship, one of these orders came from the White House in Washington DC.

By the end of the century the annual output of Dewar's whisky had reached 1,000,000 gallons. The London offices were now concentrated at Dewar's Corner on the right bank of the Thames near Waterloo Bridge. It was an historic site, for it was one of the last places where round cannonballs were made by dropping molten lead down a long shaft.

This Shot Tower, which was later to figure in the 'Festival of Britain', had long been a prominent feature on the Thames landscape, and the House of Dewar put it to good use by displaying on it one of the largest electrical signs in London. The design covered almost the whole height of the tower and portrayed a bearded Highlander with a bottle of White Label in his left hand and a glass in his right. The coloured lights were so worked as to make the Highlander raise his glass frequently and cause his kilt and beard to stand out as though swayed by the wind. To ensure that everyone should know what whisky the genial

Highlander was drinking, the name Dewar stood out in huge letters above his tam o' shanter. For many years the sign gave a never-failing thrill of pleasure and anticipation to millions of Londoners including jaded members of Parliament, and there was general regret when the foundations of the tower were declared to be unsafe and the hardy Highlander had to be removed from his exalted position.

The name of Dewar not only figured on neon signs; it soon appeared in Burke and Debrett. On the accession of King Edward VII, Tommy Dewar received a knighthood. In 1907 John Dewar was given a baronetcy. In 1916 he was raised to the peerage and assumed the title of Baron Forteviot of Dupplin, a fine estate with a famous trout-loch which he bought in 1910 from the Earl of Kinnoull. The new baron did much to embellish and improve the estate. The next Earl of Kinnoull was to make history by becoming the first hereditary peer to join the Labour Party and by marrying Miss May Meyrick, daughter of the London night club queen who enjoyed a short but prosperous reign at the 'Forty-Three' and 'The Silver Slipper' after the First World War.

As Tommy Dewar also received a peerage in 1919, the House of Dewar had become a major dynasty in the kingdom of whisky. The two brothers had travelled far and fast. In less than a quarter of a century two grandsons of a Perthshire crofter had transformed a small whisky-merchant's shop into a vast world concern and had made huge fortunes for themselves.

Their success was the reward partly of the opportunity which an expanding market presented to them and partly of their own ability. The brothers lived in a capitalist age in which competition was fierce and money-making was the hallmark of success. In character the one was the opposite of the other, but together they were a formidable combination of Scottish dourness and Scottish dynamic energy. Lord Forteviot was a home Scot and remained at home to make good whisky. Quiet and serious in manner, he excelled as an organiser and administrator. He was in the best sense of the word a good man, with an enviable reputation for fair dealing and a fine record of public service. As Lord Provost of

Perth he not only made The Fair City fairer but also put its tangled finances into good order. As Liberal member for Inverness, where he twice defeated the Mackintosh of Mackintosh, he served two terms in the House of Commons. His heart, however, was always in Perth and in his Dupplin estate and, when he died in 1929, the city mourned him not only as a benefactor but as a citizen whose special Scottish virtues were an example which, though few might follow, all admired.

In contrast, Tommy Dewar was the complete cosmopolitan with a magnetic personality and an innate ability to get on with all sorts and classes of men. No-one took liberties with John Dewar. When he became Lord Forteviot, he remained Lord Forteviot. His brother, even after he was raised to the peerage, was Tommy Dewar to thousands who had never met him. After he made his fortune, he blossomed into an English country gentleman at Homestall in Sussex. Quick to realise the business advantages of a connection with the sporting world, he spread his activities over a wide field. He was one of the first men to own a motor car. He became a patron of association football and was the donor of the Dewar Shield which in the great days of the Corinthians was the annual trophy for the match between the best amateur club and the leading professional team of the year. Racing, however, was his chief hobby, and the Homestall stud produced some splendid horses, including 'Abbot's Trace', a famous sire whose offspring won stake money, exceeding £250,000, and with which his heir and nephew, John Arthur Dewar, won the Derby in 1931, just 14 months after his uncle's death. At Homestall he bred almost every kind of animal from goats and greyhounds to Shetland ponies and Sealyhams.

In all kinds of sport he had, as well as a long purse, a lucky hand. His first venture in coursing was the purchase of a greyhound called 'Winning Number'. He bought it mainly on account of its name, paid a £10 note for it, ran it in the Waterloo Cup and won! He honoured his debt to Fortune by including a greyhound in his coat-of-arms. And yet for all his love of sport the favourite hobby of this human dynamo was painting.

He also acquired a considerable reputation as a witty and genially cynical after-dinner speaker whose aphorisms were eagerly noted and borrowed by less gifted orators. These 'Dewarisms', commendably short, were full of worldly wisdom. 'Do right and fear no man; don't write and fear no woman' expressed the view of a confirmed bachelor. Nor did he spare mere man. 'The motor car has done away with horses, but not with the ass' was one of his favourites. Sport inspired its Dewarisms in 'golf is not necessarily a rich man's game; there are plenty of very poor players', and worldly cynicism was expressed in 'the biggest lies are told on gravestones', an aphorism which is quoted to this day and has a place in several anthologies.

Tommy Dewar also took a serious part in public life. Early in his London career he served on the London County Council and at the age of 33 became Sheriff of London. Three years later be entered Parliament as Conservative member for St. George's in the East. Always a master of time, he was perhaps at his best in his private room at Dewar House in the Haymarket, where the London offices of the firm have been situated since 1908. He made it a social centre not only for the whisky trade, but also for distinguished visitors from all parts of the world. He himself was the magnet which attracted them, and in his lifetime there were few celebrities from Prime Ministers to Prima Donnas who did not drop in to have a drink and a chat with him. No man understood better the value of publicity to the whisky trade, and from his fertile mind sprang most of the ideas which have made Dewar's advertising famous throughout the world. Tommy Dewar it was who devised the sign on the Shot Tower at Dewar's Wharf and who, after a visit to Gilbert and Sullivan's *Ruddigore*, conceived the idea of 'The Whisky of His Forefathers', the most popular of all Dewar advertisements. In this picture a Highland chief is seated drinking whisky in his dining room, and, while he daydreams, his ancestors become alive and stretch out their heads from the portrait to the bottle.

Neither Lord Dewar nor his brother, Lord Forteviot, spared any expense in making Dewar House as attractive as money could make it, and today it is a museum which, quite apart from the chances of a free dram, is well worth visiting on its own merits. It contains, amongst other famous pictures, Raeburn's masterpiece, 'The McNab', for which Tommy Dewar gave 25,000 guineas; the Chantrey bust of Sir Walter Scott, and the worn and much bescribbled tavern table on which Robert Burns wrote many of his poems.

I must add that, if Tommy Dewar made London and Sussex his homes, he never forgot his native city. Today Perth owes to him the freehold of Kinnoull Hill which commands one of the most inspiring views in all Britain.

By the time he was 50 Tommy Dewar had probably more friends and acquaintances than any other man in London, and when he died in 1930 thousands mourned him. Unlike most countries England tends to worship money and ignore its poets and authors who, as Sir Alfred Duff Cooper once said, occupy a place in the social ladder somewhere between the parson and the schoolmaster. Of Thomas Robert Dewar it can be said that he owed his popularity far more to his own attractive personality than to his possessions.

Like most of the successful whisky magnates, Tommy Dewar, in spite of the hospitality which he showered on others, was an abstemious man. I remember one occasion when two friends of mine, then comparatively young men, were playing bridge against Tommy Dewar and Alec Edward, another Scottish whisky magnate. The younger men were offered whisky and took it. Dewar and Edward drank nothing. After a third glass had been offered and taken, Dewar turned to his two opponents:

'Young men,' he said, 'you're drinking too much. You'll ruin your health.'

'And where would the trade be, Lord Dewar, if we didn't drink?' replied my special friend.

Tommy Dewar put his cards down, looked at Edward for a moment, and said quite seriously:

'Alec, there's something in what that young fellow says.'

Of the numerous members of the Dewar staff who have contributed to the unbroken success of the firm I shall mention only two names. First must come Peter Menzies Dewar. Though born in Perthshire, he was no relation of the Dewar brothers. Joining the firm as a mere youth, he soon made his way to the top and both in England and abroad consolidated the work which Tommy Dewar had begun. A man of strong personality, he was a superb picker and trainer of young men. For 25 years he travelled the world. Then, after the deaths of Lord Forteviot and Lord Dewar, he became chairman of the company. Apart from angling, he had no outside interests of any kind. He lived entirely for Dewar's. Indeed, it might be said that he died for his firm, for he continued to work long after most men would have abandoned the struggle. A serious affection of the arteries had lost him both his legs, and towards the end of his career his sight had almost gone. But with large dark glasses he made a pretence of reading his letters. The pretence was quite unnecessary. Loss of sight made no difference to him. His memory was prodigious, and his knowledge of the whisky trade unrivalled. A man with a big heart and a strong but kindly nature, he belonged to a type of Scot which is in some danger of disappearing for, to quote another Dewarism, 'too many people are miserable today because they are unable to obtain the things which their forefathers never had.'

Secondly, I must mention the late Alexander John Cameron, because to him the House of Dewar owes the ingredients of its world-famous 'White Label'. I have already explained how the blending of grain and malt distillations completely altered the taste of whisky. There are many stories of the origin of blending, including one fabricated legend that the first blender was John Dewar, the founder of the firm, who discovered the art by mixing the remains of nearly empty kegs. In point of fact, the history of blending goes back many years before the rise of the House of Dewar. It began with the mixing of single malt whiskies of different ages made at different times of the year from the same pot-still distillery. This process was known as 'vatting' and, with the birth of the patent-still grain distillery, it developed into the blending of malt and grain. Crude as the first mixings may have been, blending today has become a fine art, for whiskies are like the breeding of pedigree stock. They cannot be crossed indiscriminately. Like must be mated with like, and only time and the most careful selection can ensure a happy creation. Of this art Alexander John Cameron was a pioneer and the first genius.

CHAPTER EIGHT

The Walkers

MY WALK SHOULD BE A JIG.

FOR OUR next whisky magnate we must leave Perthshire and go to Ayrshire. It is a county of soft climate and hardy men who combine a practical genius for invention with a fine taste for serious literature and philosophy. Nor must I fail to mention their keen interest in politics. Independent and radical in their views, they know their facts, and dismal defeat awaits the Parliamentary candidate who comes unprepared to an Ayrshire town. The bubble of his complacency is soon burst, for the locals have a sturdy contempt for the type of oratory which seeks to mask ignorance. The miner reads his Marx, and I remember vividly how at question time after a lecture on the Soviet Union which I gave a few years ago, a local shoemaker tested my knowledge with a persistence which was the more effective because he was studiously polite and apparently open to conviction. I did not succeed in persuading him that he was wrong, but we had a pleasant talk after the meeting, and I left with considerable respect for his skill in debate.

Shrewd and thrifty, with an innate dislike of waste and extravagance, Ayrshire men have their feet firmly planted on the earth, and their share of worldly success has been great in relation to their numbers. Ayrshire is the country of Bruce and Burns, of Boswell, and George Douglas Brown, the author of *The House with the Green Shutters,* of John Galt, and John Macadam, the pioneer of modern road-making. In Ayrshire John Knox at the age of 60 married the 17-year-old heiress of Ochiltree and Richard Cameron the Covenanter was slain, 'leaving his name to a religious sect and to a renowned regiment in the British Army'.

Hard in business but generous in hospitality, the men of Ayrshire have as profound a knowledge of the legend and ritual of whisky as any Highlander. Within its borders are celebrated the most keenly attended of all the annual Burns Dinners, and at Kilmarnock was published the most famous and today most prized edition of the poet's works. It was therefore fit and proper that Ayrshire should make its material, as well as its spiritual, contribution to Scotch whisky.

The opportunity and the contribution came when, in 1820, John Walker established himself as a grocer and wine and spirit merchant in King Street in the Royal Burgh of Kilmarnock. The little town was then in the very heart of progress, for it was the centre of the most important Scottish coalfields, and here in 1812 the first railway in Scotland was laid down in order to enable the output of coal to be handled quickly. A private concern, it ran from Kilmarnock to Troon. The promoter was the Duke of Portland, who owned most of the mines. With that railway I have a family connection, for my great-grandfather and my grand-uncle were factors to the Duke and had a supervising control of the construction.

John Walker, the son of farmer forebears, had his full share of Ayrshire grit and thrift. His capital was tiny and his business small and purely local. British trade, however, was beginning to expand after the Napoleonic wars, and in 1843 the opening of the railway from Glasgow via Kilmarnock to the South gave a fillip to local business. For the first 30 years John Walker's progress was only steady and, although it provided a living, gave no indication of the fortune that was to come. Indeed, in 1852, Mr Walker was faced with stark ruin. On the 4th of July of that year a terrifying thunderstorm struck the whole district, for a cloud burst on the moor 12 miles to the north of the town and swelled the Kilmarnock Water into a raging torrent which left devastation and disaster in its course. The town was flooded to a great depth, and, like many other Kilmarnock shopkeepers, John Walker lost all his stock. He was not insured, and, as he watched the flood working its havoc, he hesitated long before deciding whether he could carry on or try his luck in another country. Grit, however, prevailed over caution, and by hard work he set his business going again.

Five years later he was joined by his son, Alexander, a man of immense energy, vision and ability, who in his later years bore a striking resemblance to Andrew Carnegie, the Dunfermline poor boy who became steel king of the United States. In those days Scots prized education more than money, perhaps because they regarded education as the high road to material success. Be this as it may, John Walker, cautious and hard-hit as he was, had given his son a thorough business training in Glasgow.

When Alexander joined the firm, it was still in a very small way of business, and the only warehouse for the stock was a cellar less than 60 feet in length. With his advent came the change from local retail business to wholesale trading. The advance was slow and gradual. It began with the wooing of English visitors. Kilmarnock itself had a national reputation for carpet-weaving which attracted many English buyers. Well-plied by John Walker, they soon acquired a taste for whisky. They took the taste and, doubtless, several bottles back to England, where Scotch was beginning slowly to replace French brandy and Irish whiskey, and spread the fame of Johnnie Walker.

In this development the more dashing Alexander played a larger role than his father. He was also interested in export to other countries and took his share and his risk in the 'Adventure Merchant Business' which was then popular among Scottish businessmen. Based mainly on Glasgow, the business took the form of a joint venture in which a group of Scottish manufacturers and merchants consigned their various wares to a merchant vessel. Through the captain or an agent at the port of destination the owners of the vessel sold the goods at the best price obtainable and, after retaining a fixed percentage to cover freight and services, remitted the balance to the Scottish firms.

This form of business had the advantage of enabling the Scottish merchant to remain at home and to dispense with the heavy expenses of maintaining large agencies abroad. It was, however, not wholly suitable for the expanding trade in whisky, and Alexander Walker, now the sole head of the business, opened his offices at 3 Crosby Square in London in 1880. He was a year behind James Buchanan and four years ahead of the Dewars. Like them, Alexander understood the art of personal advertisement. When he went to London, the only form of transport for a big businessman on his rounds was a 'growler' or a hansom cab. On his London visits Mr Walker made use of a specially built phaeton drawn by two superb ponies. It attracted the desired attention and increased the still more desired orders.

Six years after the opening of the London offices the business had prospered so well that Alexander Walker was able to bring in his two sons, George Patterson Walker and John Walker, and to turn the firm into a private limited liability company under its present name of John Walker & Sons Limited.

In 1889 Alexander Walker died in the full flush of success and as the real creator of 'Johnnie Walker' has a high place among the pioneers who created the world empire of blended whisky. He was succeeded in the business by his third son, Alec, who, according to the customary progression of Scottish success, had received a better education than his father and, indeed, his elder brothers, for he had been trained as a lawyer with one of the best legal firms in Ayrshire and as a whisky expert with Messrs Robertson and Baxter, the well-known Glasgow distillers and blenders.

In 1890 George Patterson Walker became chairman and in the same year James Stevenson, who later was to make a name for himself as a government administrator, joined the Kilmarnock staff. Then a mere youth, Stevenson was Kilmarnock born and bred. Within 25 years these two men, together with Alec Walker, were to raise the firm of John Walker & Sons to the lofty position of the largest blenders and bottlers of Scotch whisky in the world. Progress now leapt forward with rapid strides. To safeguard its own supplies of whisky, the firm bought distilleries including, of course, a Strathspey malt distillery at Knockando. In 1897 the Birmingham branch was opened, and James Stevenson went south to take charge of it. In 1902 the capital was raised from £70,000 to £210,000, and in 1907 the London office was moved to premises, more in keeping with the firm's increasing prosperity, at Dunster House in Mark Lane.

In 1908 the firm achieved its greatest success in advertising, and, like most triumphs, it was favoured by chance. In that year the firm enlisted the services of Tom Brown, then the leading black-and-white artist, for the design of a poster. As a source of possible inspiration he was given a portrait of the founder of the firm. In a few minutes Brown produced a thumbnail sketch which the directors recognised at once as a winner. It was enlarged immediately and given the now world-famous caption of 'Johnnie Walker — born 1820, still going strong'. The poster has been used ever since and has been a big factor in increasing the sales of the firm's whisky. Even today advertising experts say that it stands alone in its universal appeal.

In another respect 1908 was an outstanding year in the history of the firm, for it saw the transfer of James Stevenson to London. There his dynamic personality and his administrative ability soon made a deep impression on the minds of the leading politicians including Mr Lloyd George.

For the six years between 1908 and the outbreak of the First World War the history of John Walker & Sons was one of rapid expansion, and the firm's only anxiety was the speed of its success. Four other great concerns, in Dewars, Buchanans, Haigs and Mackies, were competing for the same market. Known with Walkers as the 'Big Five', they were suspicious of the increasing power of the Distillers Company Limited and not only had remained outside it, but were considering an amalgamation of their own huge interests. For this purpose negotiations between Walkers, Dewars, and Buchanans began in 1909 but broke down finally in June 1910.

Meanwhile, John Walker & Sons continued to consolidate and strengthen their position by the acquisition of bottle factories and the extension of warehouse storage for their huge stocks. In 1912 the capital was doubled, and George Patterson Walker, Alec Walker and James Stevenson were appointed joint managing directors.

By the time that war broke out the sales of 'Johnnie Walker' both abroad and at home had increased to such an extent that the directors were compelled to consider the relations of stocks to restricted output. Almost immediately the supply of whisky became a serious problem and by the end of 1915 the firm was forced to stop all sales of bulk to England and to restrict the sales of certain qualities of bottled whisky.

During the war the firm lost the services of James Stevenson and Alec Walker, both of whom had been summoned to the Ministry of Munitions by Lloyd George. Big businessmen who enter government service in wartime are not infrequently failures. More often than not they are driven to frenzies of frustration by the tangles of red tape which surround them and soon resign in disgust. Others again accept the frustration and become more tape-minded than the permanent official. There are some brilliant exceptions, and among these James Stevenson was outstanding. He was a born administrator and he quickly adapted the speedier methods of big business to the slower procedure of officialdom.

He went from success to success, organising the Ministry of Munitions by areas and co-ordinating the numerous activities which came under its control. Indeed, whenever there was confusion or muddle in the various departments concerned with supply and ordnance, Lloyd George's remedy was: 'Send for Stevenson', and Stevenson came, looked and more often than not conquered. He continued to serve the Government during the early post-war period and as Commercial Adviser to the Secretary of State for the Colonies devised the Stevenson Scheme for the restriction of rubber production in Malaya and Ceylon. He also organised, and made a great success of the British

Empire Exhibition in 1924. For his services he was rewarded, first, with a baronetcy and in 1924 with a peerage. It was typical of his character and his attitude towards life that for his coat of arms he chose as its prominent feature a high explosive shell erect with the motto 'Carry on'. Stevenson carried on beyond the limits of his own strength. His death in 1926 at the early age of 53 was as great a loss to his country as to his firm.

The difficult conditions which the First World War created for the whisky trade continued into the post-war period. In 1919 whisky stocks were low and, although Prohibition had closed the American market to the Scottish distillers, supplies were quite inadequate to meet the demand. In spite of the raising of the duty to 72s. 6d. per proof gallon in 1920, the big firms recovered quickly, and after celebrating their centenary in 1920, John Walker & Sons was floated as a public company in 1923 with a total capital of £2,760,000 divided into £1,260,000 of ordinary shares and £1,500,000 of cumulative preference shares.

In the same year John Walker & Sons, in conjunction with John Dewar & Sons and W. P. Lowrie & Co., of Glasgow, bought both the shares and the whisky stocks of James Watson & Co., a large and prosperous Dundee concern, and divided them between the three firms.

The recovery of the big firms is best illustrated by the production of John Walker & Sons. Restricted to 1,000,000 proof gallons per annum in 1919, it had increased to 2,200,000 proof gallons by the end of 1924.

From then on Sir Alec Walker, who had been knighted for his war services, was to be the guiding hand and genial boss of John Walker & Sons. The youngest of the third generation of Walkers, he had been born with a silver spoon in his mouth, and as a whisky expert was never regarded by his staff as the equal of the self-made men who had concentrated all their energies on blending and salesmanship. Nevertheless, Alec Walker was a remarkable man and certainly the most erudite of all the whisky magnates. If there was no subject of which he was the complete master, there was an amazing number of matters on which he could speak with enviable knowledge. More of a lawyer than a merchant, he loved to harangue his staff, sometimes at great length, and, as one possessing authority, did not like to be interrupted. On one occasion, soon after the First World War, he was addressing his chief lieutenants on foreign exchange, at that time an engrossing subject because fortunes were being made and lost on the trembling currencies of Europe. A young Ayrshire man, to whom Sir Alec had given his chance in life, was among the listeners. Trained under a famous economist, he found it hard to swallow all Sir Alec's theories and, eager to show his knowledge, ventured to voice a contradiction. Sir Alec looked up and paused until his audience stiffened into silence. Then, looking at his interrupter, he said:

'Young man, if you know as much about foreign exchange as you think you do, you have no business to be here. You should be making a fortune.'

The rebuke was merited. To most bosses, especially if they are big in mind as well as in position, it is right and sometimes profitable to say exactly what you think when you are alone with them. It is always a blunder to contradict them when other people are present. I have made the same mistake myself and have profited by it. So did the young man. Today, thanks to Sir Alec's backing, he is himself a considerable figure in the whisky world.

With increasing age, Alec Walker retired to Troon where he was a well-known figure both on the golf course and in the clubhouse. His geniality had mellowed, and he became a great raconteur who loved to sit and talk of the old days of the whisky boom. Though kind, he had considerable dignity and was never a man with whom one could take liberties. There were occasions when, in spite of his inclination to be prolix, he could be as terse as any Scot. Before one Open Golf Championship at Troon he sent a message inviting the great Hagen to meet him at the club. Delighted by this mark of recognition, Hagen dressed for the occasion and arrived at the appointed hour.

'Ah, Hagen,' said Sir Alec, 'I understand that, contrary to the rules, some of your compatriots have been removing the brushwood, and practising from the championship tees. I'd be grateful if you will see that this does not happen again. That's all.'

Visibly impressed, Hagen withdrew without even a dram of Johnnie Walker to help him on his way.

Sir Alec died peacefully at Troon in May 1950. He had been playing golf a few days previously. He had enjoyed a pleasant life and had outlived the other whisky magnates who had made and kept the fortunes of the boom days.

CHAPTER NINE

James Buchanan

A MAN MUST MAKE HIS OPPORTUNITY, AS OFT AS FIND IT.

ONE OF the most famous blended whiskies in the world is 'Black and White'. The story of its origin and ultimate triumph is the life story of James Buchanan, to me the most attractive personality of all the whisky barons.

Born in Canada in 1849 and brought back to Scotland when he was a year old, James Buchanan began his business career at the age of 14 as an office boy in a shipping firm in Glasgow. He was engaged for a period of three years at a salary of £10 for the first year, £15 for the second, and £20 for the third. It was a busy time for shipping firms, for the war between North and South was raging in the United States, and Glasgow ships were earning large profits by running the Northern blockade and supplying the South. Very soon, under pressure of this active business, the young Buchanan was doing the work of an adult clerk. In his contract his office hours were from 9am to 6pm, but rare were the days when, after a sandwich, he did not return to the office and work on till 10pm or later. For this work he received no extra pay. Realising that the experience which he was acquiring would be valuable, he was a willing horse.

Nevertheless, he was sore about the salary and, when he had fulfilled his contract, he decided to leave and join his brother, who was a Glasgow grain merchant.

In his new work he acquired that knowledge and love of hay and horses which later in life he used to great advantage as a breeder and racehorse owner. Finding no outlet for his ambition in Scotland, he went to London in 1879 as agent for Charles Mackinlay & Co., the well-known whisky merchants and blenders. The story goes that, after doing reasonably well in London, Buchanan came back to Scotland and asked for a partnership in J. & J. Ainslie, one of the oldest and most successful whisky firms in Leith. The request was regarded as cheek, and in 1884 Buchanan returned to London, set up on his own account, and founded as sole proprietor the firm of James Buchanan & Co., at 61 Basinghall Street, a gloomy thoroughfare of which I have dismal memories when the Department of Overseas Trade was established there at the end of the First World War.

To the newcomer London offered no bright prospect of success. He had little or no capital. Although the public was beginning to develop a taste for Scotch whisky, he found that the Highland and Lowland malt whiskies held a virtual monopoly of the limited market.

James Buchanan was undismayed. In Mr W. P. Lowrie of Glasgow he had a good friend from whom he obtained stocks of whisky both in bulk and in bottle. His best assets, however, were his business acumen and his own personality. At that time most of the Scotch whisky sold in London was obtained in bulk direct from a malt distillery, and each malt distillery produced a whisky of different character and flavour. Summing up accurately the chances of the market, Buchanan made up his mind to provide in bottles a blended Scotch whisky sufficiently light to please the palate and to satisfy the stomach of the Sassenach. Above all, he determined that it must be constant in quality and flavour. Having found his blend, he marketed it under the name of 'Buchanan' in a black bottle with a neat white label.

This was the origin of Black and White. Now the problem was how to sell it, and fortunately for himself Jimmie Buchanan in his own special manner was an even better salesman than Tommy Dewar. I have a friend, the best angler that I know, who enhances his skill by approaching the Highland rivers, with their background of brown hill and moor, in a battle-dress of his own design. In his approach to the London whisky buyers James Buchanan possessed the patience of the angler, and dressed for the part as well. A tall, lean figure of a man, with well-set eyes, finely chiselled nose, firm chin, carefully parted red hair, bushy eyebrows, and heavy moustache, he made his first appearance in London in a beautifully cut frock coat, high single stick-up collar, pearl tie-pin, orchid in buttonhole, glossy top hat, and malacca cane. But for slightly prominent ears, he could have passed for a blue-blooded aristocrat. Both face and figure revealed strength of character and the indefinable magnetism of charm. The fine clothes made a fine exterior, but there was a real man inside them.

Many are the stories told of his ingenious efforts to capture the London whisky trade. Some are perhaps legendary, like the story of the dinner-party at a leading hotel where, after ordering a table and an elaborate dinner, Buchanan and 11 friends arrived in full evening dress, sat down with great éclat, and asked for Buchanan's whisky. When the head waiter expressed his regret, the 12 rose as one man and, after a horrified chorus of 'What! no Buchanan's!', left the room.

Strictly true, however, are the stories of his more subtle and profitable approaches. His first task in London was to choose an accountant for his firm. In Mr Newsom Smith he found not only an accountant but also the chairman of the United Music Halls Company which then owned most of the leading London variety theatres. Through Newsom Smith, Buchanan obtained the contract for the music-halls. Then he marked down another magnate of the licensed trade who was also proprietor of an hotel. Buchanan made a point of dining every night in the hotel restaurant. He soon made the acquaintance of the proprietor but never mentioned whisky to him. After four months the proprietor, who had discovered what Buchanan's business was, became interested.

'You're in the whisky trade,' he said. 'Why have you

never asked me for an order?'

Buchanan replied modestly: 'You are so big and so important that I didn't like to sound you until you knew me better.'

Again he got his order.

No man understood better the maxim that more flies are caught by honey than by vinegar. He received another big order from a widower — also a prominent man in the trade — by taking his two daughters to the Cinderella dances organised by his Burns Club. The two girls who had recently returned from a convent school in Brussels were delighted, and the father gave practical expression to his own pleasure in an order for 5000 gallons of whisky.

The serious-minded young Scot with the perfect manners had a genius for making himself known by methods which invited attention without displaying ostentation. One useful magnet of attraction was his famous buggy with red-spoked wheels. It was drawn by a beautifully bred black pony which he drove himself with a dapper 'tiger' behind him.

Within a year of setting up his own business in London he obtained a contract for the supply of his whisky to the House of Commons. It was the first triumph of 'Black and White'. Indeed, this special brand, if not made entirely for the House, was put up in its black bottle and white label in order to appeal by its discreet appearance to the dignified Members of Parliament of those days. Indeed, at first the title 'Black and White' was printed in small letters and was minor to the main label of 'House of Commons'. Soon, however, so many people began to ask for 'that black and white whisky' that 'Black and White' became the sole label and the words 'House of Commons' were deleted.

In 1889 Buchanan received a welcome present for his fortieth birthday when in open competition at the Paris Exhibition his firm was awarded the Gold Medal for Scotch blended whisky. By 1895 he had acquired a sufficiently large share of the London trade to enable him to enter the export market. Like the other whisky magnates, he himself travelled the world in order to choose and appoint his agents.

He was now on the flowing tide of expansion, and in

1898 he brought off his most daring coup when he bought the Black Swan Distillery in Holborn. The site was not only of a high business value but also of great historic interest. On it had stood the Swan Inn, perhaps the most renowned of all the coaching inns of London. From its friendly sign started the York coach which on many occasions Dick Turpin honoured with his special attention. Towards the last quarter of the eighteenth century the inn was acquired by a Mr Langdale who converted it into a distillery. The original building had a short life and in 1780 a sensational end. That year is memorable for the Gordon Riots when Lord George Gordon and a fanatical mob, after setting fire to Newgate Prison and many other neighbouring buildings, concentrated in full force before the Black Swan Inn. Drunk with frenzy, they were now determined to satisfy their thirst with real liquor. Attacking the distillery at once, they quickly forced entry, while Mr Langdale escaped by a back entrance. Smashing open the casks, they flung themselves on the flowing liquor. Presently fire broke out, and in a second the burning spirit was running in streams of flame. At first the seething men and women paid no heed, and those in front were pressed forward by the rearguard in its desperate efforts to obtain its share of free alcohol. Many drank the burning liquid and reeled half in agony and half in delirious intoxication. Before any semblance of order could be restored, scores had died from drinking red hot spirit. Others again who were inside were handed out, alight from head to foot with burning spirit, to perish in the streets.

The horrible tragedies and human degradation of that night are described in *Barnaby Rudge,* and not even in the Blitz has London witnessed such scenes of horror.

The distillery's losses amounted to £50,000, most of which had to be borne by Mr Langdale himself. By way of compensation the Government rebuilt the distillery which since that night of orgy had changed hands several times. In 1898 it was owned by Sir Allan Young, a rich businessman who was interested in yachting and made something of a name for himself by financing Polar expeditions.

For some time James Buchanan had been looking for a more spacious office for his business. Once his mind was made up, he never wasted a minute in following up decision with action. A hint from one of his agents was therefore enough to send him off at once to his solicitor. Their conversation was brief:

'I want you to buy the Black Swan Distillery for me today,' said Buchanan.

'Good God,' replied the solicitor, 'I — you — cannot do that.'

Buchanan insisted. Off went the solicitor to see Messrs Nash, Field & Withers who acted for Sir Allan Young. In 24 hours the deal was concluded, and Buchanan had bought the distillery for £87,000. He had no idea where he was to find the money but within a week he had arranged the finance and embarked on his rebuilding scheme. Mr Leonard Martin, the architect, then a young man, but later to achieve fame, was given a free hand. The building which he designed not only satisfied all the requirements of James Buchanan but added distinction and grace to the drabness of Holborn. The house, built in Bath stone, is still the head office of the firm.

The year 1898, in which James Buchanan bought the Black Swan Distillery, was also to bring him perhaps the greatest compliment to his ability and integrity of character. I have already told the story of the Pattison failure which brought ruin and disaster to Scottish speculators. After the collapse a Scottish syndicate was formed to take over the Pattison stocks of whisky and to keep the business going. Soon the members of the syndicate came to London to see Buchanan. They begged him to undertake a valuation of the Pattison stocks. Buchanan was not interested and, pleading pressure of business, advised them to find a home Scot for the job. The members of the syndicate returned to Scotland, but in a few days were back in Holborn. The Scottish banks who were backing the syndicate would accept no other valuer than Buchanan. The members of the syndicate offered Buchanan any fee he liked if he would pull them out of the difficulty. He named a high figure and made the valuation.

In the end the reconstruction scheme fell through because the Pattison failure was irredeemable, but the members of the syndicate, although hard hit, were bound, and at once offered to pay Buchanan his full fee. James Buchanan refused to take it and said that, if the members wished to give anything for his services, he would be well content if they would send a cheque for £50 to the Wine and Spirits Benevolent Association.

Cynics may say that this gesture was another piece of clever advertising, but there was a finer fabric than the tough texture of mere business ability in James Buchanan's character. Many Scottish whisky firms, some by their own folly, but others through no fault of their own, were in temporary financial difficulties after the Pattison failure. In the second category was the firm of W. P. Lowrie & Co., whose chairman had befriended and helped James Buchanan when he first came to London. Now without fuss and, indeed, without any request from the firm, James Buchanan saw his old friend through his troubles.

The 15 years from 1899 to 1914 were to bring an immense and prosperous development of Buchanan's business. Branches were opened in the large provincial centres of England and in Paris. Royal orders for 'Black and White' or 'Red Seal' came repeatedly from King Edward VII and from the Prince of Wales, later to be King George V.

With the huge expansion in the whisky trade Buchanan, like the other whisky magnates, was careful to ensure his supplies and stocks of whisky by acquiring and building warehouses, bottling factories and distilleries. Among the malt distilleries which he acquired was Convalmore, one of the seven distilleries which make the little Banffshire town of Dufftown the most concentrated area of distilling in the world.

In 1903 James Buchanan & Co. was incorporated as a limited liability company with an issued and paid-up capital of £850,000. There was no public issue, and the bulk of the shares remained in James Buchanan's hands. In 19 years he had created from almost nothing one of the largest one-man businesses in the world. Viewed from all aspects, it was and remains a remarkable achievement. Among Buchanan's acquisitions was the firm of W. P. Lowrie & Co. which he took over in 1906, when Mr Lowrie retired from business, and reconstructed with an authorised capital of £500,000. During the First World War James Buchanan & Co. went through the same difficulties as the other great whisky firms. Huge orders had to be cut down and new orders refused. Eventually Government rationing of orders on a basis of 50% of the 1916 supplies helped to put a check on a situation which was rapidly becoming chaotic.

Like the other members of the 'Big Five' of whisky, Buchanan's had held aloof from the Distillers Company which it still regarded with some suspicion. In April 1915 a big advance was made when Buchanan and Dewar formed an amalgamation on their own with a capital of £5,000,000. It was indirectly the result of the uncertainties arising out of the war.

The big distillers could not see their way clearly, for there seemed no end to Government restrictions and impositions. In 1917 came the new blow when the strength of bottled whisky was reduced to 30 under proof, and the duty raised to 30s. per proof gallon. To the distillers the rise seemed ruinous, but gradually taxation was to make them shock-proof, and the increase of the duty to 50s. in 1919 was softened by the brighter prospects which the end of the war unfolded.

For a time shortage of supplies continued, and customers protested loudly against the restrictions. Expansion, too, was severely limited by the Volstead Act and the enforcement of Prohibition in the United States. Gradually, however, the big firms adapted themselves to the situation. If the tempo of development was slower than in the great years from 1880 to 1914, it was steady. The 'Big Five' had done marvellously well and could afford to relax and, replete with fortunes and honours, to allow younger men a larger share in the control of the trade.

In 1903 James Buchanan, an enthusiastic volunteer from his early days, had made friends with Lord Roberts and had been much influenced by that eminent soldier's warnings of the dangers which threatened an unarmed and unforeseeing Britain. One of the first men to give practical effect to Lord Roberts's advocacy of rifle clubs, he founded the Buchanan Rifle Club in 1905 and was one of the few employers of those days to give ample opportunities for training to his staff without counting their period in camp as part of their holiday. When the First World War started, the House of Buchanan provided the country with 454 men, many of them trained rifle shots and all volunteers. Throughout the long struggle Buchanan himself was a determined and generous supporter of all measures to increase the efficient conduct of the war and to improve the lot of the soldiers.

For his services he was made a Baronet in 1920. Two years later he was elevated to the peerage and took the title of Woolavington of Lavington. At the time there was a widely circulated story that the peerage was offered to him by Lloyd George in return for a large contribution to L.G.'s party fund and that, having little faith in the promises of politicians, Buchanan had signed his cheque 'Woolavington'. The story is a legend with no foundation of truth, but it serves to illustrate the reputation which Buchanan then enjoyed as a man over whose eyes not even the wiliest politician could pull the wool of flattery, much less of deception.

The new peer was 73. He had retained his long slender figure and looked more than ever like a retired diplomat. Indeed, his features bore a distinct resemblance to those of that most aristocratic-looking of ambassadors, the late Sir George Buchanan, whom I served in Russia during the First World War.

It was, too, as an aristocratic sportsman that Spy, the famous cartoonist, portrayed him in *Vanity Fair in* 1907. The picture shows him still dressed as immaculately as in his youth. The red hair is now sand-coloured. The moustache, a little ragged but as long as ever, dwarfs the cigar which protrudes from the half-concealed lips. He wears a white butterfly collar with hunting pink tie and waistcoat and a brown coat from the breast-pocket of which dangles the finest of white linen handkerchiefs. The riding-breeches are a magnificence of sponge-bag check; the neatest of riding legs are enclosed in the softest of buttoned leggings. The slender right hand holds a hunting-crop; the left is delicately inserted in the breeches pocket so as to show a neat white strip of shirt below the well-cut sleeve.

Supporting all this elegance is the tall, graceful figure as slim and as erect as ever. James Buchanan, as a very rich man, is still the same dandy who came to London to initiate the unsuspecting English into the mysteries of whisky and in the process to make his own fortune.

Like Lord Dewar, Lord Woolavington bought himself a fine estate in Sussex and was able to indulge his love of horses with full heart and purse. At Lavington Park he took up racing and blood-stock breeding with great zest and in the same year in which he was made a peer he won the Derby with 'Captain Cuttle'. He repeated his triumph in 1926 with 'Coronach'. Both horses were bred at Lavington and, to their owner's great pleasure, both had as sire his famous stallion, 'Hurry On', which as a racehorse was never beaten.

If horses were his first love, dogs came second, and early in his career he won more useful successes with them than with his horses. From his busiest days he found time to visit dog-shows, and in 1892 he returned from a visit to Scotland with a negative of the three champion Highland terriers of that year. On the journey back to London it occurred to that fertile imagination of his that a picture of the three dogs painted by a well-known artist and given the title of 'Real Scotch' would make an excellent advertisement for his whisky. The artist was commissioned at once, and the picture was an immediate success. Since then dogs have been the main feature of Buchanan's advertisements, and of course the combination of black and white has been fully developed by eminent artists employed by the firm. Indeed, some whisky drinkers have a better knowledge of dogs than of whisky. In the early thirties Buchanans received the following letter sent on to them by Dewars:

'To Messrs Dewar & Co., Glasgow

Dear Sirs,

I have very much admired your poster of two cocker spaniels, as I have one exactly like them, and should like a copy. We always drink your 'White Horse' whisky at home here.'

(The poster was of course a Buchanan advertisement. Messrs Dewar & Co's head offices are in Perth and London. White Horse is a Mackie whisky!)

The only occasion on which I have ever attempted to inspire an advertisement was when I conceived the idea of two black and white magpies with the title: 'One for sorrow, two for joy.' That talented peer, Lord Darnley, painted an excellent picture and submitted it to Buchanans. It was rejected. I imagine that the word 'sorrow' was a serious obstacle. Doubtless, too, the idea had been suggested on several previous occasions.

In spite of his age and his sporting interests Lord Woolavington remained active in business until his death in 1935, a few days before his 86th birthday. All his life he had been obliged to husband his health and was therefore a most abstemious man. Nevertheless, there was a tough fibre to his delicate constitution. In 1924 he paid a business visit to South Africa. On the return journey he broke a thigh at Madeira. So strong was his vitality and so remarkable his powers of recovery that, although he was then 75, he was able to make another business tour the next year. And neither as James Buchanan nor as Lord Woolavington did this remarkable Scot ever undertake any business without performing the leading part in it. In 1926 when the General Strike threatened to paralyse all business in England, he decided to launch an ambitious scheme of expansion in Australia where Black and White had always sold well. Acquiring a superb site, the firm built magnificent new premises which at the time represented the last word in modern equipment. Fortune favoured bold action, for the value of the site increased many times when the Australian Government erected the great bridge across Sydney Harbour. Incidentally, the first manager of the new offices was Warwick Armstrong, the subtlest Test match cricketer who has ever captained Australia.

I must mention the famous horses and vans which for over 40 years delivered Buchanan's whisky and were the delight of every Londoner of those days. They were of course the creation of Jimmy Buchanan, and no expense was spared to make everything connected with them unique in its appeal. The horses, picked and later bred by Buchanan himself, were the most beautiful of their class. Their harness was superb. The coachmen and trouncers were dressed in the picturesque fashion of the old stage coachmen. When the long line of vans assembled in Holborn, received the load of whisky, and drove off on the daily round, foreign visitors thought that they were witnessing a Victorian pageant, and even the Holborn businessman halted to turn an admiring eye before resuming, with a new gladness in his heart, his way to his office. The turn-outs attracted a great holiday crowd at the annual parades of the London Van Horse Society on Whit Monday. Both the society and the parades were inaugurated by James Buchanan, and at them and at other shows his horses won many prizes.

Alas! the march of time and the muddled maze of London's traffic have banished the old order, and in 1936 to the sorrow of horse-lovers, and they include 90% of Londoners, Buchanan's announced the withdrawal of their horse-vans and their replacement by motor traffic.

James Buchanan was the kind of man who would have made a success of any enterprise to which he chose to turn his mind. His achievement was great, not because he made a fortune for himself, for in its acquisition the times in which he lived favoured him, but because from small beginnings he had built up a vast concern which gave fair and generous treatment to all its employees and which was conducted in so honest a manner that, whatever views on drink or on capitalism may be held by temperance advocates or Socialists, no word was ever whispered against the character of the man who created it. Later in the firm's history he had very able lieutenants like Edward Stern and William Harrison, but his was the hand that laid the foundations and his the brain that on them built the main edifice. Nor did success spoil him. He remained to the end a quiet and modest man.

In his old age James Buchanan liked to give advice to young men. The gist of it was that work never hurt any man and that character was worth more than brains. James Buchanan had both brains and character, and few men have worked harder.

CHAPTER TEN

The Haigs and the Mackies

THE CHOICE AND MASTER SPIRITS OF THIS AGE.

THERE remain to complete my portrait gallery of the 'Big Five' of whisky the House of Haig and the House of Mackie. Of the two, the older in pedigree and the longer established in the trade is the House of Haig. This Border family is one of the most ancient in Scotland and can trace its descent back to the twelfth century. Its fame is established in the couplet known to every Scot:

> *Tide what may betide*
> *A Haig will be laird of Bemersyde.*

The family's connection with whisky is also ripe in age. It began with Robert Haig, the second son of the seventeenth Laird of Bemersyde. He left Bemersyde in 1623 and, having learned distilling in Holland, set up a still near his new home at Throsk in Stirlingshire. The business was confined to local trade, and its course ran smoothly but for one incident which gives Robert Haig a place in the history of whisky. In those days there were few rules concerning the distillation of whisky, but many governing the observation

121

of the Scottish Sabbath, and on January 4th, 1665, Robert Haig received an unpleasant surprise when he was summoned to appear before the Kirk Sessions for working his still on a Sunday. He pleaded not guilty. In point of fact, the evidence showed that the culprit was a servant lass who had profited by her master's absence to make a few pints of alcohol for herself and her friends. The word of a Haig being above suspicion, Robert, upon a promise of Christian carriage for the future, escaped with a rebuke. The record of his appearance before the Sessions is preserved to this day.

When by the middle of the nineteenth century Coffey's invention of the patent-still had created a rapidly increasing demand for factory-made spirits, the Haigs, represented then by three firms, had already a large interest in whisky with distilleries at Seggie, Kincaple, and later at Cameronbridge, Fife. Together with the Steins, they were the first distillers to work for the English market, and this early connection with England resulted later in the erection of the Hammersmith Distillery which was built by a Haig.

Of the Haigs the big man was John who, in addition to the determination common to all Haigs, possessed a vision that was rare among his competitors. He was one of the first distillers to enter the two Trade Arrangements by which a small group of distillers sought to regulate prices and sales, and, when as a result of the comparative failure of the Trade Arrangements the Distillers Company came into existence in 1877, John Haig of Cameronbridge Distillery was one of the six constituent firms.

The amalgamation caused some personal inconvenience to John Haig, for in accordance with the D.C.L. regulations he had to remove the trading office of his firm from Cameronbridge to Markinch some three miles away. To obtain the use of a suitable bonded warehouse, John Haig, Sons & Co., amalgamated in 1882 with David Smith & Co. of Leith. The Leith bonded warehouse was retained until 1892 when a new warehouse was erected at Markinch and all the firm's activities were concentrated there. Two years later John Haig & Co. was floated as a limited liability company and registered in Edinburgh on April 4th, 1894.

From now on the firm's expansion followed the same

successful course as that of the other members of the 'Big Five'. To ensure its own supply of malt whisky the firm acquired Glen Cawdor Distillery, Nairn, in 1903. Royal orders were received, and in 1906 John Haig & Co. were appointed purveyors to the House of Lords. Firmly established in England with large offices in London and Manchester, the firm became increasingly active in the export market and before the First World War had its agents in every whisky centre of the world. The chief brands of Haig whisky are John Haig Gold Label and Dimple.

The Haigs were not blind to the sales value of advertising. 'Don't be Vague, ask for Haig' was an obvious winner, and in my youth I remember seeing in Berlin the strange but welcome sight of a smart trap with two admirably groomed Shetland ponies being driven along Unter den Linden by a magnificent Highlander in full dress. The Berliners loved it — and asked for Haig.

The 1914-1918 War caused much the same difficulties that the other whisky firms had to face and, in particular, Haigs suffered severely from the Volstead Act, for they had established a good business in the United States and were making great headway when Prohibition put a temporary end to it. However, in one respect the war was beneficial, for it enforced a closer unity of the various Haig interests in whisky, and in 1924 John Haig & Co. and Haig and Haig Ltd. were completely merged.

The Haigs were a large family, and whisky made fortunes for several of them. The foundation of this wealth began when Robert Haig installed his little still at Throsk, but the man who built the House of Haig was John Haig of Cameronbridge. Deservedly his name ranks high among the pioneers of blended whisky. He has also another claim on the attention of posterity. Thanks to his success as a distiller, he was able to send his son, Douglas, to Clifton and Sandhurst and, later, into the 17th Lancers. Whisky, therefore, can be said to have given the nation the brilliant cavalry leader of the South African War and the dour, strong-jawed Commander-in-Chief of the British Army in France during the First World War.

Edinburgh claims Field-Marshal Lord Haig as her son,

but his parents' home was Cameron House which adjoined the Cameronbridge Distillery built by his father. He was, in fact, removed there a few days after his birth, and, if he escaped being born in a distillery, he was brought up in one. At Cameronbridge he spent his childhood, his school holidays, and later, when he entered the army, much of his leave. Long before he had mastered the art of strategy, he knew almost all there was to know about whisky. His official connection with the family business dates from his 21st birthday, and he became one of the original directors of the firm when it was converted into a limited liability company in 1894. Thirty years later, with the honours and burdens of two wars heavy upon him, he was appointed chairman. From that moment until his death in 1928 he never missed a board meeting. His name, of course, was a great asset to the company, but in his diligence, his shrewdness, and his thorough knowledge of the whisky trade he brought to the business much more than the prestige of his military achievement. The Distillers Company knew very well what they were doing when they made him a director in 1922, for in those days, at least, they never appointed anyone to their board unless he was strictly worth his place on his merits as a whisky expert.

Soldiering and distilling run, or used to run, together in the Haig family. In addition to the Field-Marshal, Major John Haig, who won a D.S.O., and Colonel Oliver Haig also fought in the First World War. Colonel Haig died a few years ago. He was the owner of Inchrory, situated at the foot of Ben Avon and famed for its grouse and deer. At 80 he was a remarkably hale and active man who could walk most townsmen of half his age off their feet.

Of the four founders of the five big whisky companies whose portraits I have sketched, John Dewar senior, James Buchanan and John Walker were self-made men. John Haig was in a different category, but all four had made their fortune out of blended whisky and were the beneficiaries of Aeneas Coffey's invention of the patent-still.

Even today the man in the street thinks involuntarily of the Highlands whenever he mentions the word whisky; but it is curious that, while the original whisky has been distilled for centuries in Highland glens, the big whisky fortunes have been made in the Lowlands.

Among the 'Big Five' the missing 'Mac' is supplied by the firm of Mackie of which the great driving force in its success was Sir Peter Mackie, the man who made 'White Horse' a household name throughout the whisky world.

Mackies had been in the whisky trade for several generations. In the boardroom of the company is an old desk with a silver plate bearing the names of the partners who had occupied it in turn since 1801. On it the name of Mackie appears three times.

The first real records, however, date only from May, 1883, when the firm of James Logan Mackie & Co. was established in Glasgow. The partners were J.L. Mackie, uncle of the subsequent Sir Peter Mackie, and a Captain Graham, both of whom carried on business as distillers at Lagavulin, perhaps the most famous of the Islay malt distilleries, and also as traders in whiskies, brandies and clarets.

The Mackie family has an ancient history. When James Logan Mackie died in 1917, he was probably the senior proprietor by direct descent of house property in Edinburgh, for he retained, till his death, a house which had been conveyed to his ancestor, Alexander Mackie, Burgess of the Canongate, in 1650.

Using Lagavulin for their malt whisky, James Logan Mackie & Co. produced the blend of malt and grain whiskies which under the name of White Horse was to make the firm's fortune. Islay malt whiskies have a special rich flavour of their own and are, on this account, not so popular with most of the big blenders. The flavour is mildly retained in White Horse which is therefore easily distinguished from the Dewar, Buchanan, Walker and Haig brands.

The name, a happy choice, was taken from the far-famed White Horse Inn in the Canongate of Edinburgh. The inn had been a favourite of Prince Charles Edward's officers during the '45, and Boswell had introduced Dr Johnson to its smoky atmosphere. But, as Peter Mackie soon discovered, 'White Horse' had a far deeper significance than a connection with an inn, however strong its liquor or its historical associations. A white horse was symbolic of power and victory, of purity and high ideals. In this sense it could be traced back to the earliest Scandinavian sagas and, as Chesterton was to write:

Before the gods that made the gods
Had seen their sunrise pass,
The White Horse of the White Horse Vale
Was cut out of the grass.

By great generals, too, a white horse was regarded as lucky, both for the safety of the rider and for the favourable issue of the battle. Was there not the famous white Marengo of Napoleon and, in the very times when Peter Mackie was most active, Lord Roberts's white Voronel? All these romantic associations and superstitions were stored by Peter Mackie in his mind and turned to good use as advertising copy for White Horse. Assuredly that ancestor worship which lies so deep in the Highlander's heart had worked a miracle when James Logan Mackie, remembering the family tree in the Canongate, fixed on the name of an Edinburgh inn for his blend of whisky.

In 1890 James Logan Mackie retired and was succeeded by his nephew, Peter. The name of White Horse had been James Logan Mackie's great contribution to the firm. Now it was the lot of Peter Mackie to extend its sales. He was well equipped for the task. Born in 1855, he had been trained as a distiller at Lagavulin and had joined the firm in its early years. To technical knowledge he added energy, imagination, and a determination to succeed which, common enough in the Scotland of the last century, seems to us today ruthless in its intensity.

A year after Peter Mackie took over, the firm was floated as a private limited liability company and the famous brand, White Horse, was registered under the Trade Marks Act.

Selling White Horse was no easy task in that fiercely competitive age. The race was to the swift, and the Mackie chaser had a long leeway to make up before it could catch the other leaders. Peter Mackie, however, was born to overcome difficulties. In my own boyhood my mother never tired of telling me that with sufficient willpower a man could achieve any ambition on which his mind and heart were set. I never believed her. Peter Mackie was brought up on the same precept and did his utmost to make it come true. With restless zeal and a vivid and fertile Highland imagination, he met all counsels of caution with the phrase: 'Nothing is impossible.' By constant repetition it became a byword and a joke throughout the company's staff. It was, however, a joke which no-one dared to take lightly, and by much the same methods and acquisitions which brought fortune and fame to the other members of the 'Big Five', Peter Mackie, ably assisted by Andrew Holm, the father-in-law of the well-known Scottish lady golfer, soon spread the fame and sales of White Horse over the whisky-drinking world. By 1914, Mackie & Co. had made rapid progress, and its position in both the home and export markets was outstanding.

The war brought a temporary check to the company's success and a grievous personal affliction to its chairman. Ninety per cent of the male staff volunteered for active service, and in 1917 Peter Mackie's only son was killed in action near Jerusalem. He had been appointed to the board of directors only a few months before the war and was on a world tour when it broke out. He returned at once and joined up.

To forget his sorrow Peter Mackie plunged more deeply into work than ever. The war had forced him to scrap many ambitious schemes of expansion. When it was over, he made strenuous efforts to recover the lost ground. He bought more distilleries including Craigellachie, not far from one of the most beautiful and inspiring stretches of the Spey, which at Craigellachie village is spanned by a bridge linking the low-lying right bank to a precipitous wooded hill on the other side of the river. The bridge spans a magnificent pool which in the fierce winter of 1895 was frozen so hard that for the only time in the memory of man it gave weeks of sport and pleasure to skaters and curlers.

Simultaneously with these material acquisitions, new blood came to the board of directors in the persons of

Captain G. Mackie-Campbell, M.C., Captain G.F. Boyle, and Mr Andrew Holm, junior. Captain Mackie-Campbell and Captain Boyle were sons-in-law of Peter Mackie. Unfortunately Boyle was killed in an aeroplane accident not long after becoming a director.

Finally, in 1924 the firm of Mackie & Co. was dissolved and reconstructed under the tide of White Horse Distillers Ltd. Its biggest coup came a year or two later with the introduction of the White Horse screw cap for bottles. The innovation, which did away with corkscrews and the nuisance of unyielding or bad corks, took the whisky trade by surprise, and during the ensuing six months the sales of White Horse were doubled.

In 1920 Peter Mackie was made a baronet. If the honour was conferred on him for his success in the whisky trade, he must have been gratified, for of all the whisky magnates he was the most ruthless in his rugged individualism and the proudest of his own achievement. Amalgamations with D.C.L. or with any other group were not to his liking. As for pride in his success, he acknowledged his debt to whisky by including three ears of barley in his coat-of-arms. James Buchanan, created baronet in the same year, went one better, for although for his coat-of-arms he chose only two ears of barley, they were held fast in the sinister paw of a very rampant lion.

A man of striking figure and virile personality, Peter Mackie can best be described as one-third genius, one-third megalomaniac and one-third eccentric. Looking his best in Highland dress, he loved to parade as a Highland chieftain. Never happier than when on a moor, he became a recognised authority on shooting and was the author of *The Keeper's Book* which ran through several editions. He also played his part in politics, travelled the Empire and wrote with vigour and vision on Imperial Federation. A strong Tariff Reformer, he was for a time President of the Scottish Unionist Association.

There is a type of dynamic Scot whose mind is never happy unless it is playing with figures and blueprints, planning new inventions, and seeking to make better out of good. To this type, which has produced many Scottish triumphs of invention and not a few failures, Peter Mackie belonged. Believing that in business, as in life itself, a man must go forward or slip back, he was never content with his success as a distiller, but was always planning new ventures. As he was an autocrat, he was able to indulge them at will. Some of these postwar ventures, like the purchase of Holloway's Gin Distillery, were legitimate, for they were cognate to his whisky business. It was a different matter when he embarked on the weaving of Highland tweeds and the making of concrete slabs, although for the latter venture he found a good customer in the Glasgow Corporation. Typical, too, of his versatility, and rather more eccentric in its nature, was his entry into the milling industry. Inspired by a desire to build a race of bonnier and better Scots, he produced a flour called B.B.M. The initials revealed its purpose. They stood for Brain, Bone and Muscle. So energetically did he develop his product that soon all the leading grocers all over the country were stocking it. The White Horse staff had no choice in the matter. They had not only to stock B.B.M. but also to eat it.

I do not know what profits, if any, were made by these sideshows, but after Sir Peter Mackie's death in 1924 all these ventures were abandoned.

Inevitably there were many other men in, or connected with, the whisky trade who profited greatly during the years of expansion from 1880 to 1914. Here I shall mention only Sir James Calder, partly on account of his own considerable contribution to the development of whisky, but mainly because he was intimately connected with the whisky magnates in the days when they were building their empire. He died in August 1962 aged 92.

Sir James, the son of a timber merchant, had the good fortune and the ability to win success in several different capacities, including that of a Government official. In the First World War, he was Assistant Controller of Timber and finally Controller of Timber, and in the second war Controller of Home Timber. Realising early in life the possibilities of the boom in whisky, he floated several distillery companies. He was for many years a friend of my mother's family and often visited Balmenach. These visits ended profitably for my relations and, I hope and believe, for Sir James Calder. In 1923 the Distillers Company were eager to acquire Balmenach, and my uncle Jim Macgregor was ready to sell. The negotiations were conducted by my uncle Tom in Edinburgh. No flies came near him in business or even when fishing, and, when the D.C.L. named a price and would go no further, Tom rang up James Calder and on the telephone extracted a higher bid from him. Sir James floated the new company and later sold the distillery to the D.C.L. at a handsome profit.

A keen fisherman, Sir James was chairman of the syndicate which owns the Grimesta river in the Lews where in 1883 a Mr Naylor made the record catch of 57 salmon to his own rod in one day.

Up until his death, Sir James enjoyed good looks and superb health, was amazingly active and led a busy life between London and his two homes in the Ochils and in Norfolk. He was president of the Scotch Whisky Association and chairman or director of five breweries. I need hardly say that he was a man of vision. Doubtless, he was one of the first to realise that, while Scotch whisky was conquering the world, it would be taxed out of existence in its native country.

I have reserved for a later chapter my comments on the ethics of the drink trade, but here I may properly sum up the virtues and faults of the men whose real achievement was to create an international taste and insatiable desire for what had hitherto been a national and, indeed, mainly Highland drink. They lived in a spacious age when capitalism had a free rein and opportunity offered rich rewards to those who were able to grasp it. They made huge fortunes and kept them, as the spirit of the age not only entitled but encouraged them to do. In the process they altered the taste of whisky, and this was and is still regarded as their greatest sin by the malt distillers and by the Celtic enthusiasts of malt whisky. However regrettable this may be, it is at least open to doubt whether malt whisky by itself would ever have conquered the world and whether the blender-magnates, by taking a proportion of malt whisky, did not, in fact, benefit the pockets of the malt distillers even if their palates were offended.

Nearly 100 years ago, a French cynic, when asked to define capitalism, quoted the coup of a horse-coper who bought a horse for 2400 francs and sold it two days later to the Empress Eugenie for 24,000 francs. There were evils enough in the Scotland of those days: glaring inequalities of wealth, harsh employers, and deplorable conditions of housing, and today we are paying not only for two World Wars but also for the sins of our grandfathers who, with money to spare, imported the cheapest labour they could find and housed the immigrants in hovels.

But it was not in the manner of the French horse-dealer that the whisky magnates made their fortunes. In their day they stood in the first rank of good employers, treating and housing their staff well and inspiring a loyalty which was generously rewarded. They had no desire to fill their pockets by fleecing the public. On the contrary, their policy, determined partly by keen competition but also by sound common-sense, was based on low prices and high sales. It was a paying policy because it was the right policy, but none can deny that it was pursued with efficiency. The magnates took a genuine pride in the quality of their products and, whatever may be the respective merits of blended and pure malt whiskies, they succeeded in producing brands which won the approval, not only of the medical profession, but also of millions of city dwellers who had never tasted whisky before.

It is irrational and unfair to blame them today for making money and keeping it. They can be judged only by the standards of the times in which they lived, and by those standards their reputation for fair dealing is high. Still more foolish is it to condemn them for not being Socialists and for not sharing their wealth with others. Thirty-four years of Socialism imposed by force on another country has shown that the dictatorship of the proletariat can enslave the workers in a manner that even the most rapacious capitalist would never have dared to imitate and that, until mankind can free itself from its three curses of jealousy, cruelty and lust for power, society will always be divided into two classes of bosses and bossed.

Nor must the ability of the whisky magnates be under-estimated. They were born in an era when Scotland was producing men of the highest quality. Because the country was poor, many Scots were forced to emigrate to countries where the harsh but solid virtues of Presbyterianism stood them in good stead and raised them to pinnacles of success in politics, finance, and public administration. Those Scots who remained at home climbed the ladder of fierce compe-tition. For this struggle the whisky magnates were well equipped both by character and by innate ability. Their merit was not so much that they came to the top as that they remained there and extended its vista.

At the peak of their success they were rewarded with high titles, and at the time there was some criticism and even sneers. England, however, has always showered hon-ours on big money, and in this respect justified Napoleon's dictum that the English are a nation of shopkeepers. Moreover, the English nobility has never at any time hesi-tated to marry money, and it is by this transfusion of new blood and by the elevation of successful men in all walks of life that it has escaped the effete decrepitude which through inbreeding has overtaken other European aristocracies.

In this hierarchy of merit the whisky magnates were by no means unworthy of their place. They brought to their new rank brains, financial ability, and a capacity and willing-ness to take their share in public affairs. Few, if any, of them desired to shine as social butterflies. They remained hard-working and abstemious, preferred seclusion to notoriety, continued to attend to their business, and spent their scanty leisure quietly in their shooting lodges in the Highlands. It paid them handsomely to make good whisky. As for their money, they used it wisely and without waste, contributing generously to good causes and perpetuating their names by permanent bequests to the land of their birth.

They were favoured by the times in which they lived, for today the State rightly ensures a more equitable distribution of wealth and by high taxation prevents the accumulation of vast private fortunes. The First World War sounded the knell of rugged and often ruthless individualism; the Second has destroyed big fortunes, probably for ever.

One fact remains to be stated. Social prejudice did not sanction the bestowal of honours for the making of good Scotch. The whisky magnates received their titles for their public services. Only two of them, Lord Woolavington and Lord Stevenson, have been immortalised in the *Dictionary of National Biography*. Lord Woolavington is described as a philanthropist and racehorse owner and Lord Stevenson as an administrator.

PART III

War, Prohibition and Dollars

TELL THEM WHA HAE THE CHIEF DIRECTION
SCOTLAND AN' ME'S IN GREAT AFFLICTION,
E'ER SIN' THEY LAID THAT CURST RESTRICTION
ON AQUA VITAE;
AN' ROUSE THEM UP TO STRONG CONVICTION
AN' MOVE THEIR PITY.

BURNS

CHAPTER ELEVEN

Amalgamation

MAN WANTS BUT LITTLE DRINK BELOW
BUT WANTS THAT LITTLE STRONG.

MODERN wars, which reward neither the victor nor the vanquished, shake the foundations of every edifice of our complicated civilisation and affect constituted authorities and institutions as well as individual lives. In this respect the First World War gave the first warning to Europe. While Continental monarchies tottered to their doom, the minor dynasties of whisky were being undermined at home.

With a suddenness difficult to realise at the time, August 4th, 1914, dawned on a prosperous community whose first reaction was the foolish slogan of 'business as usual'. Business was to continue, but in a new and strenuous form. The war brought the almost unchecked prosperity of the whisky barons to a sudden stop and caused a series of complex troubles to the whole trade. Its cumulative effects were to sap the strength of the independent malt distilleries, to foster amalgamation, to bring the control of the trade into fewer hands, and to increase the duty on the product and the taxation of the distilling industry. Government interference began from the start of hostilities, for in whisky the

Treasury discovered a milch-cow with a wonderful yield and since then has never ceased to milk it. It was therefore doubly fortunate for the whisky cow that the Distillers Company Limited was already in existence and that in its managing director, Mr W.H. Ross, the company had a man of strong character and outstanding ability.

The first economic consequence of the German invasion of Belgium was the cessation of all supplies of yeast from the Continent, and without the D.C.L.'s yeast the bread supply of Britain would have been seriously endangered. The United Yeast Company, formed by Ross in 1899 after long experiments to find the best process, was able to fill the gap, and it is interesting to recall that the first yeast produced for D.C.L. was made in the Haig Distillery at Cameronbridge. In war it is the task of the soldier to destroy in order that others may be able to create. In the First World War Field-Marshal Haig, who was a whisky expert before he was a captain, was both a destroyer and a creator.

Ross's foresight in developing yeast as a by-product of the D.C.L. stood him in good stead in his negotiations with the Government, for early in the war the whole whisky trade was seriously perturbed by the rumour that Lloyd George, then Chancellor of the Exchequer, had been 'nobbled' by the Temperance Party and was preparing to close down the distilleries and introduce prohibition. When the rumour proved to have more solid foundations than mere gossip, Ross packed his bag and went to London to see Lloyd George. He soon found that the Temperance Party had made some impression on the Chancellor. Lloyd George, in fact, had been moved by two arguments: first, the damaging effect of alcohol on the production of the British industrial worker and, secondly and more important, because more romantic to his Celtic mind, the prohibition of vodka in Russia, which the Tsar had introduced by a special ukase as soon as the war started.

It is curious that Lloyd George should have been impressed by the example of Russia, for later many expert observers were to attribute the success of the Russian revolution to the prohibition of vodka. I was in Russia throughout the First World War and wrote numerous reports on the morale of the people. I cannot support the argument that prohibition was one of the major causes of the revolution, although I admit that discontent was fanned by the contrast between the privileges of the upper class and the restrictions imposed on the masses. Prohibition in Russia produced much the same effects as it was to do later in the United States. To the rich vodka was available at a price; the poor could not afford it and addicts poisoned themselves with wood alcohol and denaturalised spirit. The only indirect evidence that prohibition accelerated the revolution is the fact that, as soon as they had established themselves securely, the Bolsheviks reintroduced the sale of vodka. In the Second World War Stalin was to tell Sir Anthony Eden in Moscow, when Voroshilov was carried out feet-first from an inter-Allied banquet, that his generals fought better when they were drunk.

Be this as it may, Lloyd George in 1914 was more than halfway along the road to a dry Utopia, and Ross found him in a difficult mood. Patience and exemplary equanimity of temper had made him the best negotiator in Scotland, and he listened with sympathy to Lloyd George's arguments. Then quietly and modestly he presented his own case. The prohibition of distilling would put a stop to the manufacture of yeast, and without yeast how was Britain to be supplied with bread? He pointed out the almost countless uses of alcohol and its by-products for war purposes: for high explosives, for anaesthetics, for coating the wings of aeroplanes.

When he left the Chancellor, the battle was half-won. But it was not over. The advocates of temperance had not abandoned the field, and in 1915 the distillers were summoned to a conference with the Government. Representing officialdom were Mr Walter Runciman, President of the Board of Trade; Lloyd George, who had just become Minister of Munitions; and several experts, including Sir Arthur Tedder, then a high official of the Inland Revenue who had begun his career as an excise officer in Glengyle Distillery, Campbeltown. At the meeting the members of the Government took a grave view of the situation. On account of the submarine menace every bushel of grain would have to be conserved for food. Many distilleries would have to be closed. Nevertheless, they stopped short of prohibition, although the production of whisky was heavily curtailed and the product itself rationed. For this act of mercy the distillers were grateful, although their thirsty customers were not.

At the conference table Sir Arthur Tedder was helpful and conciliatory. Thirty-five years later the D.C.L. remembered his services when in 1950 they appointed his son, Marshal of the Royal Air Force Lord Tedder, a director of the company. It was the first time in its history that the D.C.L. had selected as director a man who had no special knowledge of the trade or of finance.

In 1915 the Government introduced the Immature Spirits Act. Its origin was curious and was to have an unforeseen effect on the fortunes of the 'Big Five' of whisky. The right hand of Lloyd George at the Ministry of Munitions was James Stevenson, the able director of John Walker & Sons, and Stevenson was able to convince his chief that cheap new whisky was responsible for the increased drunkenness which was causing the Government so much anxiety. On Stevenson's advice Lloyd George brought in the Act which compelled distillers to keep all whisky in bond for two years. At the end of 12 months the bonding period was extended to three years.

The effect of the Act was to create a short market, and whisky which cost from 3s. to 4s. 6d. a bottle went to 12s. 6d. and higher. When, as we shall see later, the 'Big Five' sold out to the Distillers Company in 1925, it was on the basis of the enhanced price.

As Minister of Munitions, Lloyd George needed the distillers, who had now become useful allies, and at the conference he suggested that they might produce acetone, a product for which hitherto we had been dependent on the United States. The distillers agreed at once, and six distilleries started to manufacture acetone. Only two had reached the stage of production by 1917 when the entry of the United States into the war ensured a plentiful supply and relieved Britain of all anxiety.

But in many other respects the distillers made a powerful contribution to the war effort. To give only one example, the Distillers Company Limited delivered approximately 50,000,000 gallons of proof alcohol to the Propellent Supplies Branch of the Explosives Department of the Ministry of Munitions.

The Armistice of 1918 found a Britain thirsty for whisky and the big suppliers short of stock. The war had broken down most of the barriers of British reserve and, in particular, had given a new freedom to unmarried girls. In the past gin had been the tipple of the matrons of the working classes and appeared in many a music-hall joke as mother's ruin. Now for the first time young girls learned to drink strong liquor, and gin itself became the principal ingredient of the cocktail which before the war was almost unknown in Britain. The demand for whisky was also insistent, and British whisky drinkers were fortunate in that the pound sterling was reasonably firm and that the United States had introduced Prohibition. Otherwise, British customers would have fared worse than they did.

Although the restrictions on the supply of whisky continued into the postwar period, they were gradually relaxed. The Government itself was a large holder of stocks of spirit, for the Ministry of Munitions had been left with 3,500,000 proof gallons of industrial spirit and a similar quantity of potable spirit. Early in 1919 the Government entered into an agreement with the distillers whereby the latter undertook to dispose of the potable spirit on behalf of the Treasury and to allocate it among customers on a pro rata basis. The distillers also agreed to find a market for the industrial spirit at the current price and received from the Government a commission of 2% on sales.

By and large, the war increased the demand for whisky and therefore stimulated the revival and expansion of the trade in the postwar period. On the other hand, it dealt almost a deathblow to the independent distillers of malt whisky. Since they did not manufacture industrial alcohol, many of them were forced to close their distilleries during the war. The financial losses which they suffered and the uncertainties of the postwar situation induced them to sell, and during the next 10 years the vast majority of them succumbed to the tempting offers of the Distillers Company Limited.

As far as whisky was concerned, the most important effect of the war was to strengthen the hand of the D.C.L. which, by creating subsidiary companies for the development and control of the numerous by-products of alcohol, was well on its way to domination of the whole whisky trade. As soon as the war was over, it entered boldly into a policy of financial expansion and experiment, the extent of which can be gauged from its rapid increases of capital. In 1919 it was raised to £2,500,000; in 1920 to £4,000,000 and in 1925 to £6,000,000. A portion of this capital was used for the purchase of malt distilleries, more and more of which were taken over by the Scottish Malt Distillers Limited, a subsidiary company of the D.C.L. already formed in 1914 for this very purpose. Still more capital was expended on acquiring control of the export markets, and in 1924 a new subsidiary, the Distillers Agency Ltd., was registered to take over the Export Branch of D.C.L. Two years later the Distillers Corporation (Proprietary) Ltd. of Australia and the Distillers Co. of Canada Ltd. were formed, the D.C.L. holding a controlling interest in the Australian Corporation and an equal interest in the Canadian.

Undeniably the policy of the D.C.L. was bold and showed a remarkable confidence in the future of whisky and in the purchasing power of the whisky public. Taxation had fallen heavily on the industry, for in 1920 the duty on whisky was raised to 72s. 6d. per proof gallon. Less than 100 years before it had been only 2s. 3d. per gallon for what the older generation of today still considers a far nobler whisky. Malt distillers rubbed their eyes, wondered who could buy whisky at 12s. 6d. a bottle, and consoled themselves with the reflection that, after all, they had not fared so badly by selling their distilleries.

There was, however, no dismay in 12 Torphichen Street, Edinburgh, behind whose dignified and unpretentious stone walls sat William Ross, the genius of the Distillers Company. His dream had not yet been fully realised. The dream was ambitious, but personal gain had no part in it. A pioneer in amalgamations, he had long foreseen that the whisky trade would never prosper until prices could be stabilised and reckless competition reduced to reasonable limits. As he was to say later, nothing was further from his mind than a monopoly formed for the purpose of cornering a commodity to the detriment of the public. What he envisaged was an amalgamation of interested parties whose purpose should be to produce and distribute an article at a reasonable price and by which the benefits should be divided fairly among consumers, workers and shareholders. He never attempted to acquire a concern merely for the sake of acquiring it. Confident that in time all would come to him, he knew how to wait, and, one by one, the malt distillers had made their way to Torphichen Street. The 'Big Five', however, were still outside, and Ross's dream could not come true until they had joined the amalgamation. Patience and the march of events were the factors which would ensure their co-operation.

The 'Big Five', who had weathered the storm of the war and were expanding in the same manner and by the same means as the D.C.L., were a formidable and difficult group to bring together. The bosses, men of strong personality, were autocrats who mistrusted each other even more deeply than they suspected the designs of the D.C.L. Their own success had been achieved by rugged individualism and bitter competition, and, tied by their nature to these methods of commercial warfare, they had hitherto regarded every form of amalgamation not only as a limitation of their individual power but also as a threat to their financial interests. Until the war they had never learned to consider the good of the trade as a whole, but had conducted their business in a spirit of rivalry in which the capture of a new market by one firm was a triumph over the other. It was a kind of clan warfare in which the 'Big Five' were Macdonalds, Macgregors, Maclarens, Frasers and Camerons who not only quarrelled among themselves but also regarded the D.C.L. as Campbells, with William Ross the Macallum More, ever avid to acquire property. In such an atmosphere quarrels were inevitable, and in the past there had been quarrelling. It was Ross's view that, if it continued, the whisky industry would be ruined.

Fortunately, the lessons of the war had not been ignored by the 'Big Five', who had realised the advantages of combination in the trade's negotiations with an ever-encroaching Government. They had also experienced the crippling effects of government restrictions and were now faced with a new problem. With the shortage of stocks which the war had caused, they were eager to secure regular supplies of grain and malt whiskies for their business. They had watched with suspicion the increasing power of the D.C.L. and, appreciating its strong position and enhanced prestige in government circles, quickly realised that, if the D.C.L. wished to be unscrupulous, they themselves might suffer. They were faced with two possible policies: to build more distilleries of their own or to amalgamate.

The first member of the 'Big Five' to see the light of amalgamation was Haig. In March, 1919, D.C.L. acquired control of Haig and Haig, John Haig & Co. being run as a separate subsidiary unit until 1924 when Haig and Haig Ltd. and John Haig & Co. Ltd. were completely merged under the aegis of D.C.L.

Walker, Buchanan, and Dewars, however, still held aloof, though the merger of Buchanan and Dewars in 1915 showed the change that the war had worked on individualist mentality. In 1925 William Ross, who had waited long enough, invited the three great firms to discuss amalgamation. They accepted the invitation, and at last William Ross had them where he wanted them — round the conference table. The negotiations, however, were difficult and, even after Ross had persuaded them that amalgamation would benefit the whole trade and therefore themselves, there were long discussions regarding the terms and conditions on which the amalgamation should be concluded. The problem was also complicated by the fact that at the time the shares of the D.C.L. stood at 42 to 43 shillings whereas Buchanan-Dewars and Walkers were quoted on the Stock Exchange at approximately 10 shillings higher. As always, Ross, the master negotiator and diplomatist, found the solution by accepting the value of the shares as the basis for the merger and suggesting that each party should submit its balance sheet and profit and loss account to the joint auditors of the four companies. The accountants got down to work at once and in two and a half months the deal was through.

Old rivalries die hard. In accepting the agreement the three members of the 'Big Five' made one stipulation. It was that William Ross should be chairman of the Distillers Company. Although a man of singular modesty, whose only ambition was to secure the good of the industry, Ross accepted the chairmanship. It was his just reward. He had handled the negotiations with consummate skill and, as Lord Forteviot was to say later, no man but William Ross could have made a Dewar and a Walker sit down at the same table together.

To meet its increased commitments, the capital of the Distillers Company was raised immediately to £15,000,000. On the new board of directors the former D.C.L. representatives were reduced from 13 to 10; of the new directors, the Buchanan-Dewar group supplied eight and the Walker group three.

Two years later the Distillers Company acquired control of White Horse. All the 'Big Five' were now in, and in 1925 the Distillers Company celebrated its fiftieth anniversary. At the two dinners, in Edinburgh and London, an array of whisky peers and magnates, supported by celebrities from the political world, paid tribute to the company and to its chairman who had done so much to create it.

Malt distillers and connoisseurs who believe that malt whisky is alone entitled to the name of whisky have said that the success of the Distillers Company was won by finance at the expense of the individual quality of the product. In point of fact, its achievement in uniting the whole industry was a triumph of combined power against Government interference. Only a united industry could make a stand against excessive taxation and other burdens imposed by the State. It was this knowledge that won the day and induced the 'Big Five' to throw in their lot with the D.C.L.

The Distillers Company began as an amalgamation. It has continued amalgamating ever since, and today its ramifications are spread over a vast field of industrial enterprise, directly or indirectly concerned with alcohol. The range of products and the uses which they serve are gigantic, and the number of companies owned or subsidised by the D.C.L. is well over 100. It has huge sums invested in the plastics industry and in chemicals and solvents. It owns or controls 60% of the production of Scotch whisky, two-thirds of Britain's gin production. About four-fifths of Britain's output of industrial alcohol is produced by British Hydrocarbon Chemicals Limited, which is owned in equal shares by D.C.L. and the British Petroleum Co. Ltd.

The company owes much of its success to William Ross, its greatest chairman, and no account of Scotch whisky would be complete without the story of his career which runs on the familiar lines of 'From log-cabin to White House'.

Born in Carluke in Lanarkshire in 1862, William Ross was the son of a farmer. After attending the local school he went to George Watson's, the largest of the Scottish public schools and famous for the number of ministers which it has supplied to the British Government and for its many rugby footballers who have worn the blue jersey of Scotland.

Unfortunately, William Ross had no time to win either scholastic or athletic distinction at Watson's, for he left at the age of 15. There was no money to spare in the family, and he went straight from Watson's to the job of office boy in the City of Glasgow Bank.

Eleven months later, on October 2nd, 1878, the bank failed, bringing ruin to many Scots. Without delay Ross began to look for another job. Several Scottish firms, including the Distillers Company, offered posts to members of the bank's staff. Ross sent in his application to the D.C.L., and 12 days after the bank had closed its doors he joined the company as a junior clerk.

Promotion came quickly. At the age of 22 he was appointed accountant and chief cashier. Five years later he became secretary of the company and in 1897 general manager. He was already the indispensable man, and in 1900 he was given the key-post of managing director. The appointment was the reward of hard work, an unrivalled knowledge of every detail of the distilling industry, and a complete lack of self-interest. When he came to the Distillers Company, it was barely 18 months old and he himself only 16 years of age. He made it his child, grew up with it, steered it through the difficulties of its youth, and brought it to a sturdy and vigorous manhood.

Only a strong man could have achieved so much, and Ross's character was a rare combination of exceptional strength and unassailable integrity. Six feet five in his stocking-soles, he was a fine slim figure of a man with a beard and a countenance whose austerity was relieved by the kindly expression of the eyes. The American magazine *Fortune* once compared him to Bernard Shaw as El Greco might have painted him. The description is apt, although, in truth, Ross bore more resemblance to El Greco's portrait of St. Jerome in the National Gallery in Edinburgh.

As a businessman Ross was a practical visionary far ahead of the age in which he lived. He believed in amalgamations and in research. He foresaw the coming change from individual to collective forms of organisation in our economic life and 50 years before the Socialists achieved power, he installed in Torphichen Street what today is called in official language a planning division. There was one important difference. His planners were experts in their particular industry, and not civil servants.

His business qualities were great. Courage, tact, and patience came first and were supported by a brilliant accounting brain and a remarkable memory. The courage was tempered by a proper share of Scottish caution, but when he thought he was right he was absolutely fearless. The least ostentatious of men, he cared nothing for social pomp or success in sport, and, apart from his work, his only interests were in books and in music. He made no millions. He gave his name to no brand of whisky and to the outside world, to whom Buchanan, Dewar, Walker and Haig are household gods, he remains almost an unknown figure. At the time when whisky barons were being created freely, the man who had composed their differences and added to their fortunes was offered an O.B.E.

His co-directors urged him to refuse it, but Ross accepted it without demur. It was, he said, another honour for the company.

The last 13 years of his life were tragic. In 1931, as the

result of an accident on board ship on his way to Australia two years previously, he lost the sight of both eyes. He bore his affliction very humanly. He married, as his second wife, the first nurse who tended him and, when she died, he married her successor. When his own end came in 1944, he was 82. In his will he bequeathed £40,000 to create a research institute for the study of the causes of blindness.

It is also to his munificence that Edinburgh is indebted for the covered orchestral stand and seated enclosure below the Castle rock in Princes Street Gardens. On at least one occasion stand and enclosure have been hired by a temperance society!

CHAPTER TWELVE

Prohibition

Four and Twenty Yankees, feeling very dry,
Went across the border to get a drink of rye.
When the rye was opened, the Yanks began to sing:
God save America, but God bless The King.

THE biggest blow to the Scottish distillers after the First World War was the introduction of total Prohibition by the Government of the United States. Its enactment is one of the most curious episodes in the astonishing history of the American people who, ever since the Declaration of Independence, have combined rugged individualism with high idealism in a manner frequently baffling to the rest of the world.

Local prohibition was not unknown in the North American continent. Long before 1914 there had been 'dry' states both in Canada and in the United States. When at the turn of the twentieth century Thomas Dewar arrived in Quebec, he found a Commission sitting there to consider the advisability of applying prohibition to the whole of Canada. The next day he sent the Commissioners a sheaf of detailed statistics showing the average life of various classes of drinkers. The total abstainers had the shortest lives. Next came the habitual drunkards whose average was two years

149

longer. Top in longevity came the moderates who drank nothing but whisky. Very properly he received a severe rap from the teetotal newspapers. As for local prohibition, there were means of evading it. Travelling one day through a 'dry' state, Dewar was advised by the Pullman conductor to try his luck at a store at the next stopping-place. He took the advice and without any diplomatic preliminaries asked the storekeeper for a bottle of whisky.

'Got a medical certificate?'

'No,' said Dewar with a crestfallen look which might have passed for sickness.

'See, mister, this is a Prohibition state, so I can't sell it, but I reckon our cholera mixture'll about fix you.'

Dewar bought the bottle and read the instructions: 'Cholera Mixture: a wine-glassful to be taken every two hours.' As the shape of the bottle seemed very familiar to him, he turned the bottle round. On the other side was the label of John Dewar & Sons.

If local dryness was mainly an inconvenience which provided ingenious methods of evasion, total Prohibition was a very different matter. Introduced as a war measure in 1917, but not signed by President Wilson until after the Armistice, it was accepted with absent-minded nonchalance by the American people. When the Eighteenth Amendment, which authorised the introduction of Prohibition, came before the Senate and, later, the House of Representatives, it was passed after two of the shortest debates in the history of Congress. Ratification by the states followed with similar ease and by January 1919 the Amendment took its place in the American Constitution. The Volstead Act, which laid down the measures by which Prohibition was to be enforced, went through with no effective opposition and, although President Wilson vetoed it, the Senate lost no time in passing it again. Even the most thirsty anti-prohibitionist can understand the readiness of the American people to accept restrictions in 1917. The entry of the United States into a European war had been made on a wave of Spartan idealism. Alcohol was a menace to the American effort, and to be dry became the patriotic duty of American men and especially of American women who had not yet experienced the delights of cocktail orgies and chain-smoking. In this atmosphere of austerity the Anti-Saloon League, which had long been active, had no difficulty in obtaining the abolition of the saloon, the American equivalent of the British public-house. The saloon, the drinking refuge of men only, had never been popular with American wives. During the war, too, the teetotallers were well-organised and very active. The 'wets' were apathetic.

These minor war restrictions followed an ordinary pattern which was familiar to other belligerents. What was extraordinary was the fervour with which the American people accepted Prohibition *after* the war. For total Prohibition did not enter into full force until January 1920, and at first it swept the country like a best-seller.

The light-hearted enthusiasm with which it was first welcomed was the more inexplicable because the American people, more mercurial in temperament than any other, were no longer in a frame of mind to accept restrictions of any kind. The war had brought almost fabulous wealth to the United States. Victory had consolidated the gains. The country was bulging with new-rich, seeking new ways and opportunities of both spending and increasing their money, and, in the same light-hearted manner that they accepted Prohibition, they suddenly turned against it.

Illicit distilling began almost at once, and, aided by a buoyant Stock Exchange and an unprecedented 'boom', the bootleggers entered into their paradise. Very soon the 'speakeasy' took the place of the saloon, but with this difference: women now joined with the men in defying the law and in celebrating their defiance in strong alcohol of uncertain quality. As Frederick Lewis Allen said in his fascinating and brilliantly written *Only Yesterday*, 'under the new regime not only the drinks were mixed, but the company too'.

The ruler of the new regime was Al Capone, and under his dominion the law fell into complete disregard. Detesting the interference with their liberties, sober and high-minded Americans, who had hardly ever touched liquor before, now made it almost a point of honour not only to drink on all occasions, but also to make gin in their own bathrooms.

Never before in history has there been so flaming an example of a bad law defeating its own ends.

I myself was in the United States during and after Prohibition. I have seen much drinking in many countries, but the United States of the 'dry' period surpassed all that I had previously experienced or, indeed, that I could have imagined. It was, I think, André Maurois who said that we make a sport of war and the Americans make a war of sport. During Prohibition the American people were making both a sport and a war of drinking with all the concentrated vigour and enthusiasm which they bring to any action they consider at the time to be really serious. To the bewildered European visitor the situation was more fantastic than real, and for my own part I lived in a perpetual state of fear lest I might be drinking poison. My American friends, assuring me that they had the real stuff, plied me with 'Scotch', and my thirst overcame my caution. But only once can I remember any ill-effects.

In almost every hotel were notices announcing that the proprietors had given an undertaking to co-operate with the authorities charged with the enforcement of the National Prohibition Law. The notice made no difference. As soon as the waiter was convinced that you were not a Prohibition officer he offered you Scotch or Bourbon. The price was stiff, especially for Scotch whisky which, real or not, cost about a dollar a glass. Other hotel notices requested gentlemen 'to open their *medicine* in the bathroom'. On the shelves of every drug-store was a coruscation of hip-flasks of every size and description, and at evening parties the protuberance on the back of the men's dresscoats left me with the impression that every American had an enlarged right buttock.

The civilisation of the New World had stepped back into the pioneer period when men took the law into their own hands, and some towns advertised themselves more or less openly as 'the wettest' in the States.

Nor was the drinking confined only to the general public. Prohibition officers, poorly paid and far too few in number to control the thirst of a rampant continent, yielded not infrequently to temptation. One of the officials of the

Distillers Company who was visiting the United States at the time tells the story of a friend who was held up in his car by two Prohibition officers. Finding two bottles of whisky in the boot, they took the man to the police station where he spent the night in a cell. Brought before the court next day, he at once challenged the Prohibition officers to produce the whisky. They could not, because they had caroused all night on the two bottles. With the crushing remark: 'They must have drunk the evidence', the accused man got off scot-free, but without his Scotch.

Typical of this amazing period were the serious poems and doggerel verse written in praise of alcohol. Of the second category I quote this effort entitled *Ah, This is Love:*

There's the wonderful love of a beautiful maid,
And the love of a staunch, true man;
And the love of a baby that's unafraid —
All have existed since Time began.
But the most wonderful love, the love of loves,
Even greater than that of a mother,
Is the tender, infinite, passionate love
Of one dead drunk for another.

It is the virtue and sometimes the vice of the American people that they never stop halfway. During Prohibition they certainly went the whole length of the road.

This most puzzling episode in American history lasted for nearly 14 years during which four different Presidents of the United States held office. So far had the reaction against Prohibition gone by 1928 that, when Governor Al Smith, the happy warrior of the 'wets', stood as Democratic candidate for the presidency, his chances of success were highly rated in spite of the fact that he was a Roman Catholic. The 'drys', however, although discomfited, were not suppressed, and Mr Hoover, who was a cautious dry, was elected by an overwhelming majority. The disastrous slump which marred Mr Hoover's period of office paved the way for President Roosevelt's success in 1932. A year later he enjoyed another triumph when, rightly interpreting public opinion, he repealed the Volstead Act.

Repeal was celebrated by a week of frenzied indulgence. I was in New York for the occasion and was a minor victim of the prevailing exuberance. After a sumptuous dinner, for which, for the first time since 1920 the Harvard Club brought out again its famous glass, I had to lecture to a distinguished audience in the magnificent but rather solemn hall which always reminds me more of a church than a club room. It was a full evening-dress affair, and I made very heavy weather with a serious dissertation on Russia when everyone was expecting me to reveal secrets or, at least, tell good stories. At my most solemn and, for my audience, most somnolent moment, a good-looking young American with a cape flung over his evening dress and an opera hat in his hand walked slowly and painfully up the aisle. He was very dignified, but also very drunk. The audience awoke and every pair of eyes was turned on the intruder. Confused and losing the thread of my discourse, I hoped and prayed that he would find a place. But no; he continued on his laborious way until he reached the dais from which I was speaking, and calmly sat down cross-legged on the floor. Fortunately he went to sleep, but I never recaptured either my own nerve or the attention of my listeners. The incident provided the material for a short story by an American author.

In time repeal brought a sharp decrease in the number of arrests for drunkenness, but did not end immediately the sale of illicitly distilled whisky or the activities of the bootleggers. When I went to Chicago soon after repeal, I sought to ingratiate myself with anyone I met by saying that, after seeing the city, I just could not believe all the stories I had heard about the lawlessness and shootings of the Prohibition period. The reaction of my acquaintances was curious. One and all immediately expostulated and insisted on carrying me off to see the hotel where Al Capone had his first headquarters and the florist's shop where three of Al's minions pumped their lead in broad daylight into the body of Dion O'Bannion, the leader of a rival gang. Although I did not doubt that the stories were true, these visits did not convince me that Chicago was anything but quiet, clean, and beautiful. I liked it and remember it with affection. Its keen, tingling air is like champagne, and it suits Scots who, in spite of the competition of a 100 different races, flourish there. My Chicago friends were amazed at my admiration. They seemed to take a real pride in their gangsters and in the wickedness of their city. I have now been there three times, and, while my view remains the same, it may reveal the danger of superficial impressions. Just as English visitors who, seeing no blood running in the gutters of Moscow streets, return full of praise for the Soviet paradise, so I, feeling no sawn-off gun against my ribs and hearing no shots, see in Chicago only the most beautiful and the best of cities.

The Americans are a young people who rid themselves of moods and fashions as easily as a healthy child shakes off a cold. It is therefore doubtful if the orgy of Prohibition has had any lasting effects on the ideals or morals of the nation. But one surmise may be reasonably risked. It is unlikely that any Government of the United States will ever renew the attempt to foist teetotalism on its people.

The effects of Prohibition on the Scottish whisky trade are difficult to appraise. The Volstead Act increased the demand for strong liquor, and throughout the whole period of Prohibition Scotch whisky retained its qualitative value. The demand for it was great, and the bootleggers made every effort to supply it. But by no means all of the supply was real Scotch. On the enactment of Prohibition the leading Scottish distillers, including the 'Big Five', regarded the market as closed and made no attempt to break the law. But there was a vast smuggling trade, and in Scotland itself there were whisky corsairs who chartered ships and sent supplies of Scotch across the Atlantic to be trans-shipped just beyond the 12-mile limit into American cabin-cruisers which ran the gauntlet of the armed cutters of the excise and Prohibition officers. Perhaps one or two small fortunes were made, but some at least of the adventurers fared badly, especially those who went to Bermuda or the Bahamas to arrange the financing of their whisky. More often than not they fell in with smart American guys and still smarter American girls and lost both their whisky and their money. One ingenious project which deserved perhaps a better fate failed when on the eve of achieving a rich reward: an attempt to defeat the American excise by producing what we should call today a dehydrated whisky and shipping it openly as a chemical. After much experimenting the process was perfected, but just after the first small consignment had safely passed the customs, the Volstead Act was repealed.

In such ways Scotch whisky penetrated the officially closed market, but the amount was infinitesimal in comparison with the total consumption of so-called whisky in the United States. Indeed, Scotch whisky probably suffered far more from the smuggling than it might have gained if not a single bottle had left the shores of Scotland, for the bootleggers, profiting by the knowledge that some real Scotch was coming into the country, increased the quantity by forging the labels of well-known Scottish brands and attaching them to doubtful liquor of American manufacture.

The main beneficiaries of the smuggling trade were the Canadians who, with their long unguarded frontier, were able to deliver good Canadian rye and also some Scotch both by land and water with comparative security. The ship *I'm Alone,* of Canadian registry, caused the one serious international incident of the Prohibition period, for, after being pursued for over two days across the Atlantic by an American excise cutter, it was sunk some 200 miles outside the 12-mile limit.

As regards the effect of Prohibition on the sales of Scotch whisky in the American market, it is, I think, safe to say that the limited supplies of Scotch, much of it bogus, and the more abundant deliveries of Canadian rye increased the taste for rye whisky. Moreover, the taste for maize whisky, which Americans call 'corn' whisky, was fostered by the illicit distilling in the United States. Reliable statistics of the illicit whisky produced during Prohibition are not available, but the amount was vast, and large quantities of industrial alcohol, estimated at 10 to 12 million gallons a year, were diverted to the manufacture of potable spirit. All of this illicit whisky was produced from patent-stills and was sold without being matured. It was potent. Indeed, new 'corn' whisky has long been honoured by Americans with the name of 'white mule', because of its powerful kick.

The salient fact is that, throughout the long period of Prohibition, Americans drank not so much for any satisfaction of the palate as for sheer 'cussedness' in protest against interference with their liberties. Defying a bad law supplied the impetus, and the question of taste or flavour scarcely arose. All that mattered was to know whether a whisky was safe or poisonous, and the discovery of a reliable bootlegger was hailed with the same rapture and enthusiasm with which a miner in the Yukon might celebrate the unearthing of a nugget. Inevitably real Scotch suffered.

Fortunately repeal brought with it a violent reaction against illicit whisky, and from 1933 to 1939 the Scotch distillers, who before the war had established throughout the States a high reputation for their product, were able to recapture and extend a market which, owing to the decline in the consumption of whisky in Britain, was of pre-eminent value.

The story that representatives of the 'Big Five' met one another unexpectedly on the first liner that sailed to New York after repeal is a legend. The Scottish distillers, however, were quick off the mark and, by skilful salesmanship, soon convinced the Prohibition-poisoned Americans of the superior qualities of Scotch whisky. That Scotch retains this special value in American eyes is proved by the following true story:

In 1950 a Foreign Office clerk, who was on night duty, was called to the telephone at four in the morning. Across the Atlantic came a raucous and indignant voice:

'Is that England?'

'Yes.'

'Is that London?'

'Yes.'

'Is that the Foreign Office?'

'Yes.'

'Well, I've been ringing up Buckingham Palace for the last two hours, but your darned operator won't put me through. What I want to know is why the heck New York's run out of Scotch tonight.'

CHAPTER THIRTEEN

Scotland's Drink

THE DEW IS HEAVY ON THE GRASS,
AT LAST THE SUN IS SET,
FILL UP, FILL UP THE CUPS OF JADE,
THE NIGHT'S BEFORE US YET.

FROM THE CHINESE

IN CONSIDERING the ethics of making and selling intoxicating liquor I confess that at various times of my life I have felt twinges of conscience. Much as I loved Balmenach, I asked myself whether the distilling of whisky was a praiseworthy enterprise or merely a means of making money out of human weakness. I think that my uncle Jim, the last Macgregor to rule over Balmenach, shared these doubts. He liked to make good whisky and to drink it, but he was no hand at selling his product.

The truth is that a good whisky salesman must be tough as well as coaxing and must expect attacks by teetotallers and temperance reformers. On his way to the United States Thomas Dewar was denounced in a Sunday address on board ship by a Scottish divine who, having studied the list of passengers, fired the following broadside: 'We have missionaries on board going to convert the heathen, and we have a heathen grog-seller on board going to corrupt the civilised to the evils of whisky-drinking, and to encourage those who are already wallowing in that degrading and pernicious vice.'

Dewar, brought up most strictly on the tenets of the Shorter Catechism, was annoyed, not at being labelled a grog-seller, but at being apostrophised as a heathen. We live in a world of divided opinions, and the main essential to its continued existence is a wise and kindly tolerance.

Today the answer to my quandary is that the making and selling of whisky remains an art, used to be a road to wealth, and continues to minister to a quenchless human need. For since the beginning of history alcohol has been both a boon and a temptation to man. The Chinese verse which, in Miss Helen Waddell's admirable translation, heads this chapter was written in the twelfth century before Christ and is almost certainly the oldest drinking song in the world.

Then there is the story of the 1000-day wine which Lin Yutang tells so beautifully in his *The Wisdom of China*. In the fourth century of our era there was a native of Chungshan who made a wine which could make a man drunk for 1000 days. He kept the secret and the wine to himself until after much persuasion he gave a sip to a local friend. After 1000 days the maker of wine said to himself: my friend must be awake now. He therefore went to the friend's house and was told that the man had long been dead. Then he ordered the family to dig up the grave and, when the coffin was opened, there was the man sitting up, and yawning. 'Oh,' he exclaimed, 'how wonderful it is to be drunk. What time of day is it?' The people who had come to watch laughed, but strong fumes from the grave went up their nostrils and made them drunk for three months.

The sentiments and longing expressed in both the poem and the legend have echoed down the ages, and the old saying, 'Abuse of anything does not abrogate the lawful use thereof', is both sound law and sound sense. The only difficulty is to decide what constitutes abuse.

It is true that the drinking habits of nations differ widely and are influenced by climatic conditions. The Mediterranean peoples drink wine. The countries of the North, where no grapes grow, need stronger spirits, and whisky, the universal traveller, is also the drink of the tropics. The English and the Germans have made a god of beer, although governments and not gods are responsible for its present lamentable weakness. Americans drink everything and Russians drink vodka, but both drink mainly for the temporary thrills of intoxication and, especially in Russia, in the competitive spirit of seeing who can drink the other under the table. In 1850 the American Consul in London gave a dinner in honour of the European exiles of the revolution of 1848. The two chief guests were the American Ambassador and Louis Kossuth, the champion of Hungarian independence. As both were very much on their dignity, the banquet was rather like a military dinner. When the two great men left, the American Consul produced a bottle of Kentucky whiskey and poured out a large teacupful for each guest. The French and Italian exiles, who included both Garibaldi and Mazzini, raised their cups and were nearly suffocated by the fumes. Herzen, the Russian revolutionary, was the only guest to drink the poison and pass up his empty cup for more. The American Consul was delighted and exclaimed ecstatically: 'It's only in America and Russia that people know how to drink.'

I do not underestimate the drinking capacity of either the Americans or the Russians. As a young man, Prince Alexis Orlov, who died in Paris in 1916, was challenged to a drinking duel. Chartreuse was the weapon, and at one sitting the Russian drank 100 glasses. These duels are a curious and unattractive manifestation of the competitive spirit and are to be explained only by Bagehot's aphorism that the greatest pleasure in life is doing what people say you cannot do.

As for the Americans, most people, I think, would qualify the Consul's boast of the 'know-how', except in the sense of drinking hard for the sake of drinking. Young nations drink with greater speed and less discrimination than the older nations, and the severest stricture on American drinking and, incidentally, on whisky was made by Thomas Jefferson who, in a letter written in 1819 to Mr de Neuville, said: 'No nation is drunken where wine is cheap, and none sober where the dearness of wine substitutes ardent spirits as the common beverage. Wine is, in truth, the only antidote to the bane of whisky.'

Very different, indeed, is, or at any rate, was the approach of the Scottish Celt to his national drink. Throughout the ages whisky has been an integral part of the Celtic civilisation and has its origin in the mists of the Highlands from which it emerged without foreign aid. It was the natural drink of a people who, however poor they might be, had never known servitude, and to whom, in the absence of other luxuries, it was indeed the water of life which gave inspiration to their songs and strength to their bodies. It was a noble spirit, a symbol of independence, to be approached with reverence, and, in spite of the changes wrought by blending, the Celts have communicated something of this reverence to the whole Scottish nation.

This approach to whisky and freedom is still maintained at Burns Nichts, especially in Ayrshire and Dumfriesshire. I do not deny that much whisky is consumed, but a lofty ritual and a deep knowledge of Burns go with it.

Take Dumfries on January 25th, the anniversary of the poet's birth. If you are the visiting guest of honour at *one* of the several dinners in the town, you arrive early in the morning, descend at the County Hotel and breakfast in the room in which Prince Charles Edward held a Council after the ill-fated retreat from Derby. If you are wise, you will ask to be left in peace till luncheon. This gives you time to see the town by yourself if the spirit so moves you. And with or without whisky it will move you. You will see the Nith — probably in noble spate in January — and you will remember the most moving of all Burns's poems:

But Nith maun be my Muse's well,
My Muse maun be thy bonnie sel'.

Then you will find your way to Burns's House where you will be received by Tom McRorie, a great character, who will show you the famous picture of 'The Mauchline Prayer' and recite the poem to you with Celtic fire. You will lunch with Dr Lindsay Carmichael, who has the love of the land he lives in very deep in his heart. Then you will make your way to St. Michael's Church where you will find the Provost arrayed in his official robes and preceded by two halberdiers. You will attend a commemoration service in the kirk and sing the metrical version of the 23rd Psalm to the beautiful Crimmond tune. From the kirk you will walk in solemn procession to the Mausoleum and lay a wreath on Burns's tomb. And it will be covered with wreaths from many Burns Clubs.

After this ceremony, tradition demands that the Committee of the Dumfries Burns Howff Club walk you down to the Globe Inn. You will be taken round its small room, and in the parlour you will be invited to inspect the window with the original pane of glass on which Burns scratched with a diamond a verse of *Coming Through the Rye*. You will be shown the room where he used to sit and drink with his friends and from which he staggered home more than once with his wame full of whisky. It is a sober reminder to you that this is the room in which you will have to speak. Then you will be taken into the tiny bar for a dram and, again if you are wise, you will stand another round and retire for a rest.

At 7.30pm you return to the Globe Inn where 100 members of the Club are now assembled. You are taken upstairs to be introduced to the chairman and to have 'just one to wet your throat'. By 8pm you are on the right hand of your chairman at a small table at right-angles to two long tables which stretch down the seemingly endless length of the narrow room, and you wonder how your voice is going to penetrate the haze of tobacco smoke which already fills the space between the heads of the members and the low ceiling.

You look at the menu and at the full bottle of whisky beside your glass. As far as the whisky is concerned, you decide that the only safety lies in keeping your glass full all the time by adding water to it. The menu is formidable: soup, Scotch haggis 'wi' chappit tatties an' mashed neeps', Solway salmon, steak and kidney pie, and sweets and cheese to follow. On the opposite page is the toast list and, including the piper and eight singers, there are 28 names. You are down to speak twice: to deliver *The Immortal Memory* and to reply to the toast of your own health. The first must be serious, but, unless you are a real expert, you will do well not to venture into too much detail about Burns. Your audience knows more about him than you do. In reply to your own health you can let yourself go and, as there are no ladies, you are expected to be a little Rabelaisian.

You will also note that there is a toast to the Croupiers. They are there, not only to rake in the cash, but also to remove from the table those that fall by the whisky way. There will be few, if indeed any.

When the 'great chieftain of the puddin' race' is brought in, there is great hilarity, and, while the chairman recites and acts the whole eight verses of Burns's fine ode *To a Haggis,* you wonder if in this jovial atmosphere anyone will listen to your carefully prepared oration, a copy of which has already been given to the local newspaper. You will be wrong. You come up early on the toast list. You are listened to with rapt attention and, if you acquit yourself well, you are given a reception that you are never likely to forget.

The ordeal over, you sit down to enjoy the rest of the long evening, and it is both instructive and entertaining. There are songs and recitations. The songs are not all good, for whisky is no elixir for tenors or basses, but an old hand like Adam Richardson will give you *A Man's a Man for a' That* as you have never heard it interpreted before. The recitations, which you fear will be wearisome, are so well delivered and acted that you are astonished how short they seem. Tom McRorie and Allan Sproat are artists, and they are acting before experts. If for one second they hesitate over a line, there are a score of voices to remind them.

When the long programme is completed, Adam Richardson sings *Happy we've been a'thegither*, and that, too, you will remember as long as you live. There is *Auld Lang Syne*. Then the members press forward to shake your hand, and, rescuing your coat, you walk back slowly to your hotel, proud that you are erect and reasonably sober, but perhaps a little relieved that at this hour of the morning there is no motor traffic.

The next morning you will try to sort out the events of the evening, and you will wonder whom you have met. And the astonishing thing is that in this gathering of Burns wor-shippers you have mixed with bankers, barristers, doctors, rich farmers, ploughmen, journalists, policemen, business-men, shopkeepers and artisans, and you will not have the slightest idea who was who. You will not have much time for reflection, for at 10 o'clock the McKerrows, father and son, are coming to take you by car to Ellisland, the farm where Burns and his wife, Jean Armour, lived for three years before settling in Dumfries. The weather has done you proud. Yesterday was wet, but the whisky you drank has killed the cold in you. Today the countryside with its white-washed farms is smiling. You have a pleasant drive to Ellisland which lies in a cup of hilly country six miles from Dumfries and off the main road to Glasgow. You approach inauspiciously by a cart road which brings you to the back of the house and the barnyard where Burns wrote his ballad *To Mary in Heaven*. You walk round to the front of the house, and below you is Nith in all its glory, with the sun dancing on its water and its left bank lined with an avenue of noble trees. You walk along the grassy path where Burns composed *Tam O' Shanter* till you come to the field where he saw the wounded hare. Mr McKerrow, one of the great-est experts on Burns, gives you the local colour, but, if you are me, your sight and your mind are on the river with its succession of fine salmon-pools, and you vow to come back in the spring.

Then you go into the side-room of the house which, through Mr McKerrow's interest and munificence, is kept as a museum. He shows you the usual exhibits: specimens of the poet's manuscripts and letters, gauger's reports, a flute — and then suddenly your eyes are riveted to two rudely varnished pieces of wood which Mr McKerrow ignores. Are you dreaming? No. You are unmistakably right. The two pieces are Burns's fishing rod. You think of the river. You see the man. And you know for certain sure that from that stream he poached with rod and line many a salmon, as almost every Scottish fisher has done at least once in his life. And you feel at once a warm affinity with this farmer-poet who unites all Scots in a great brotherhood, and you remember Balzac's definition: 'A genius has this fine quality that he is like everyone else and no-one is like him.' This is in no way true of all geniuses. It is certainly not true of Bertrand Russell who is very lovable but like no-one else in the world, but tremendously and triumphantly true of Burns who is flesh of your flesh and bone of your bone. You hear the sound of freedom and of whisky in his trumpet, and you realise that only the small nations know what freedom really means, because they have always to fight so hard to win it and to keep it.

The contrast between the approach of the Scot to whisky and that of the Anglo-Saxon to beer is admirably depicted in two short stories by writers neither of whom was a Scot. In *The Record of Badalia Herodsfoot* Kipling makes the dissolute whisky-maddened husband, Tom, murder his wife Badalia, a slum heroine who works for the church missionaries. By way of moral Kipling writes in favour of beer which 'at least clogs the legs, and though the heart may ardently desire to kill, sleep comes swiftly and the crime often remains undone. Spirits, being more volatile, allow both flesh and soul to work together generally to the inconvenience of others.'

Compare this safety-first moral with C.E. Montague's superb story *Another Temple Gone* in which the altruistic Irish Gael, Tom Farrell, sets up an illicit still in the bogs of Gartumna and produces malt whisky which is nectar come to earth. It not only makes the police sergeant blind to Farrell's flouting of the law; it gives Celtic eloquence to his tongue. 'Mother of God!' he exclaims. 'What sort of hivven's delight is this you've invented for all souls in glory?'

And Farrell replies gravely: 'It's the stuff that made the old gods of the Greeks and Romans feel sure they were gods ... There's a soul and a body to everything else, the same as ourselves. Any malt you'll have drunk, to this day, was the body of whisky only — the match of these old lumps of flesh that we're all dragging about till we die. The soul of the stuff's what you've got in your hand.'

There speaks the Celt, and of our own Scottish Gaels Neil Gunn, as I have said, can write with the same ecstasy of Scotch whisky. Who, in all humanity, I ask, could expatiate with such inspired fervour on beer?

If this argument is not sufficiently persuasive of the superior merits of Scotch, I refer you to the reactions of various nationals to over-indulgence in their particular tipple. Let us judge them by their cures. After a carouse the ancient Greeks cooled their heads with perfumes and ate cabbage. The Russians drink olive oil, and this preliminary — a wise precaution before an official banquet — is a sufficient indication of the intent and purpose of their drinking. After an orgy they eat rye bread which corrects the stomach and removes the scent of betrayal. As a remedy for a hangover, a word of their own invention, Americans eat hot milk-toast — a horrible concoction which, I assume, is supposed to act like blotting-paper. The English, who now mix their drinks, pay a morning-after visit to their chemist for a pick-me-up, and in London the army of Heppelltonians includes among its regulars both politicians and poets.

The Scot's cure for too much whisky is a little more whisky or a hair from the tail of the dog that bit him the day before, and, because whisky is a clean drink, the cure works. In these hard days English girls starve themselves in order to buy cigarettes and some strong-minded Englishmen have given up drinking for the sake of smoking. I have known a few Scots who have given up smoking in order to drink whisky but none who has sacrificed whisky in order to be able to smoke.

Admittedly, the Scot inclines to talk too much about whisky, and, when under the influence of it, to lose his modesty. He is also illogical in his attitude towards his national drink, for I think that most Scots, especially the whisky-drinkers, dislike to see their womenfolk drinking whisky. At the same time, apart from the temperance reformers, they tolerate and sometimes positively encourage them to drink such deleterious and infinitely more potent concoctions as gin cocktails laced with sweet liqueurs. This is a comparatively modern attitude, although it is not to be explained by the desire to keep a scarce product for the male sex. It is, I think, Lowland in origin, for in the old days Highland women drank whisky with their men folk as naturally as water. Why most women prefer cocktails and gin to whisky is another matter. Doubtless, they prefer sweet drinks, and, if whisky has one defect, it is an olfactory one. By its scent it betrays the drinker for a longer period than almost any other alcoholic drink.

It is also regrettably true that in the second half of the eighteenth century, and throughout the nineteenth, Scotland had an unenviable reputation for drunkenness, especially in the rapidly growing industrial centres. The fault, however, must be attributed, not so much to whisky, although much of it was bad, as to the appalling conditions in which the workers lived. Drink was the easiest escape from economic hell, and whisky, then remarkably cheap even in relation to the low wages, was the quickest road to oblivion. As Kipling has said: 'Drink is the only thing that will make clean all a man's deeds in his own eyes. Pity it is that the effects are not permanent.' Slums and poverty were not the creation of the worker. It was the misdeeds of others which drove him to cleanse his despair in alcohol.

Certainly the effects were not permanent, but they were tried repeatedly. I still remember vividly the fear that lent speed to my legs whenever I walked down Dock Street in Dundee in the late afternoon of a winter Saturday. Every third house was a pub, and every pub a vortex in which the week's wages were engulfed. As often as not, there would be a group of men and women quarrelling, fighting and brandishing bottles on the pavement. The temperance workers raged and had cause for their indignation, but in their efforts to suppress the drink trade they neglected the social conditions on which it thrived. Whisky, in fact, was the consequence and not the cause of these conditions, and had there been no whisky, man in his ingenuity would have found, as indeed he found later in such poisonous concoctions as 'Red Biddy', another anodyne for his despair.

Today the high cost of whisky has done much to remedy the evil of heavy drinking, although of course the addicts remain even if they have to display great ingenuity to obtain what they want at no cost to themselves. Association football matches provide, or used to provide, old topers with a comfortable opportunity of a free drink. At big matches fainting cases are not uncommon, and at Tynecastle, the

Edinburgh ground of Hearts, the quickest remedy was a draught of neat whisky. The old hand would wait until near the end of the game before staging his act. In a seemingly dead faint he would be passed over the heads of the spectators to the stretcher-bearers and carried to the doctor's room below the stand. After the first sip of whisky the patient would open his eyes and promptly close them again. Obviously the remedy was good but not good enough. A more generous allowance revived him. Then, timing his withdrawal to perfection, he would shuffle painfully to the stand exit, find himself a choice seat in an almost empty tram and be comfortably on his way home a few minutes before the crowd had begun to leave the ground

Alas! that such histrionic skill should now go unrewarded. The actors have played their scene too often. Today they are known to the police, to the stretcher-bearers, and to the doctor, and other and more unpleasant remedies than whisky have driven them into an untimely retirement which permits of no 'positively last appearance'.

In spite of the decrease in drunkenness the temperance movement remains active in Scotland and is particularly strong among the Free Presbyterians. Indeed, on occasions it provokes a clash between Scottish puritanism and the national characteristic of putting two pennies together so that they may stick together and grow into a tidy fortune. Some years ago a self-made Glasgow tradesman left a considerable sum of money, most of it in shares of the Distillers Company. His daughter, who inherited, was an ardent teetotaller who never ceased to plague her friends with violent denunciations of the evils of whisky. One of them, himself a holder of D.C.L. shares, took her up:

'If you hold such strong views, why don't you sell your D.C.L. shares?'

'Och, I've no need to do that. My shares are in the yeast department.'

In a very real sense the Scot's love of whisky is a natural reaction against the rigours of Calvinism which, for all its virtues, is harsh more than tender and leans towards self-righteousness rather than to grace. It is against the fleshpots of Egypt. It insists that the devil must be fought in this world in order to secure salvation in the next. Whisky is perhaps a more dangerous fleshpot than the cucumber and the melons and the onions and the garlic which the Israelites remembered from their days of bondage in Egypt. But to the Scot, born to poverty and the hard life, it was his only fleshpot and it gave him what he could not find in his gloomy surroundings: a glimpse of the mystery and splendour of existence. There was no frailty in his character to excuse his lapses. His was the rousing kind of drinking which exalted the soul and reasserted his independence. As for wrestling with the devil, he was always prepared to do his best, provided that Auld Nick won an occasional throw, especially on Saturday nights. Then, contrite with the repentance of repletion, he would seek out the minister and admit his fall.

More often than not the minister would deal kindly with him, for with the centuries Calvinism has lost its sharper edges and not every Presbyterian minister is a prohibitionist. Indeed, in the Highlands many ministers like their dram, and in my boyhood there were a few who liked it too well. A generation or two still further back there were Highland ministers who were not above buying illicit whisky or even running their own stills. And why not? Was not malt whisky the milk of the Highlands? And in what other place should a private still be but in a private house, be it manse or croft?

Not so very far from Balmenach, in slower and more peaceful days than these of our troubled times, there was a minister who had his own private still, not in his manse, but in a wood nearby. He was a good and God-fearing man who lived alone with his daughter and brought her up in the ways of truth. She had been to school and had learned that curiosity is the golden path to knowledge, and, as the still weighed heavily on her conscience, she asked her father what she must do or say if anyone questioned her about it. Solemnly the father replied: 'A lie is the greatest of all sins. My child, you must tell the truth.'

Not long afterwards the local excise officer called at the manse when the minister was working at his still.

'Where is your father?'

'Out,' replies the daughter truthfully.

'Where has he gone? I want to see him rather urgently.'

'Och,' said the daughter with just sufficient nervousness to make the gauger think that the minister had been called away on some private matter, 'he'll just be out at his still making his whisky.'

The gauger rocked with laughter at this excellent joke and, saying that he would look in the next day, left the house.

'Truth prevails' was the favourite saying of another minister, the Martyr Jan Hus, and was adopted by Thomas Masaryk for the motto of the Czechoslovak coat-of-arms. It prevailed more effectively in the manse than it does today in Czechoslovakia.

Although most Lowlanders and all Highlanders like whisky, it is a mistake to assume that Scots are connoisseurs, although, like numerous Englishmen who talk knowingly about port, many think they are. The truth is that whisky-tasting, like wine-tasting or tea-tasting, is an art which takes years of study before it can be mastered, and it is always safer to admit ignorance and ask the expert than to profess knowledge.

In this connection Dr Marr, the Grantown doctor, tells a story about Balmenach. Summoned there one day, in his professional capacity, he drove out to the distillery with the late Mr Hastilow who began life as the boots in the Grantown Palace Hotel, became the proprietor of it, and left a considerable fortune. After the doctor had seen his patient, Hastilow and he walked over to the distillery office to see George Clark, the assistant manager. They were taken at once to the sample room where unlabelled bottles of Balmenach of various ages and qualities were arrayed. Waving his hand towards the bottles, Clark said: 'Make your own pick, and I'll give you each a bottle to take away with you.'

Marr, knowing nothing about tasting, remained seated, picked out a bottle at random, and was given a dram.

Hastilow went through all the motions of the expert, opened a bottle, rubbed some whisky on his hands, and smelt them with a prolonged sniff. Then, drying his hands carefully with a clean handkerchief, he opened another bottle. Finally, after a wearisome repetition of these gymnastics, he made his choice and sat down. He, too, was given a dram.

When Hastilow had tasted his drink, Clark said to him quietly:

'You'll be a fine judge of malt whisky, Mr Hastilow?'

Hastilow smirked with self-satisfaction:

'Well, so I ought to be after all my years of experience.'

'Yes,' went on Clark, 'but you're not so good a judge as Dr Marr here. He's drinking the finest 15-year-old Balmenach. What you're drinking is some stuff I made up last night for the farmers' hare-shoot tomorrow.'

Doubtless, we Scots have drunk too much whisky and would do so today if it were handy to our taste and purse. We still make every triumph and every holiday an occasion for a 'night' and I have known even a Burns dinner justify the verse of Will Ogilvie, the Border poet:

> *When the last big bottle's empty and the dawn creeps*
> *gray and cold,*
> *And the last clan-tartan's folded and the last damned*
> *lie is told;*
> *When they totter down the footpaths in a brave,*
> *unbroken line;*
> *To the peril of the passers and the tune of Auld Lang*
> *Syne;*
> *You can tell the folk at breakfast as they watch the*
> *fearsome sicht:*
> *'They've only been assisting at a braw Scots nicht.'*

Nevertheless, whisky has made us what we are. It goes with our climate and with our nature. It rekindles old fires in us, our hatred of cant and privilege, our conviviality, our sense of nationhood, and, above all, our love of Scotland. It is our release from materialism, and I often think that without it we should have long been extinct as a race, for we should have been so irritatingly efficient that a worse persecution than the Hebrews ever suffered would have been our inevitable fate.

In *Juno and the Paycock*, Sean O'Casey makes the ruined

Captain Boyle say: 'Irelan' sober ... is Irelan' ... free.' Today Ireland is free and still not sober, and Scotland is neither wholly free nor wholly sober. Indeed, to the Scot who is not given to wasting his substance on fast women and slow horses, whisky is today his only extravagance. Everything encourages him in this national strength and weakness. In March 1951, two of the leading doctors of the United States declared pontifically that a man is a fool not to drink after 40 and should take three ounces of whisky daily to counteract the effects of hardening of the arteries. So, with the best medical opinion on his side, what is the poor Scot to do?

This, I think, is the conclusion of the whole matter. As a friend, whisky has virtues unequalled by any other form of alcohol. As O. Henry wrote in *The Lost Blend*, 'it gives men courage and ambition and the nerve for anything. It has the colour of gold, is clear as glass and shines after dark as if the sunshine were still in it.' As an enemy, there is no Scot who does not know its dangers and almost no Scottish family without its whisky skeletons. They rattle in my own cupboard, and I myself have been near enough to destruction to respect whisky, to fear it, and to continue to drink it.

CHAPTER FOURTEEN

Whisky Now

GIVE BACK THE LITTLE NATION LEAVE TO LIVE.

I MUST now return to my main narrative and recount the chequered fortunes of whisky during the Second World War, and the state and condition of its empire in the abasements and upheavals of our times.

In its effects on the trade the second war produced much the same results as the first war. Once again distillers' yeast, this time made without producing whisky, saved the nation's bread supply, and the Distillers Company, now greatly expanded, was able to provide the Government with vast quantities of industrial alcohol, chemicals, and other cognate products. The malt distilleries, however, suffered from the inevitable restrictions imposed by the war. Distilling ceased; stocks declined; increases in the duty made prices almost prohibitive, and to a nation whose demand for alcohol was stimulated by the Blitz, whisky became a rare luxury more easily obtainable in the black market or 'under the counter' than by legal methods.

Nor did the Blitz itself spare the existing stocks of whisky. On September 29th, 1940, one of the few bombs which fell in the Edinburgh area hit the large warehouse of the Caledonian Distillery near the Haymarket Station, and

1,200,000 proof gallons of whisky went up in flames. A large crowd watched the conflagration, and many Scots, fearing a drought, prayed fervently that the war would soon end. In 1941 the warehouses at Yoker Distillery, Glasgow, and at Ardgowan Distillery, Greenock, were hit on March 13th and May 7th respectively and a combined total of over 3,000,000 proof gallons perished. But except for one fortuitous blow when a German bomber dropped one high explosive bomb on Banff Distillery and caused a loss of 63,000 proof gallons, the Highlands remained immune.

These disasters to a national asset provoked some criticism and many demands for dispersal by thrifty and thirsty Scots, and Lord Rosebery, the Regional Commissioner for Scotland, was assailed by the *Dundee Courier*. Fortunately he kept a cool head, for dispersal was no simple matter, and a proposal to store millions of gallons in disused coalmines was rejected by the distillers themselves who pointed out that the stores of whisky might suffer more from such harsh treatment than from German bombs. The warehouses themselves were reasonably well dispersed. The whisky therefore remained where it was, and the final losses amounted to just over 4,500,000 gallons. The figure amounts to nearly half of our annual export of whisky, and in relation to the danger the loss must be considered as comparatively small.

Scottish whisky lovers did not fare so well, for restricted sales and the arrival of American troops with longer purses and longer thirsts soon put whisky beyond the capacity of the average Scottish pocket. With its freedom from bombs Edinburgh became a 'leave' city for overseas soldiers. The American Red Cross insisted on making visiting American soldiers its special care and, with well-intentioned but mistaken zeal sought, in a series of sightseeing tours, to combine moral and educational instruction with a policy of keeping the men out of mischief. The American soldiers who preferred elbow-lifting to brain-elevation tired quickly of the Forth Bridge and Bass Rock, jibed at the House of Knox and, preferring to admire the Castle from the precincts of Princes Street, soon found their way to the public houses. Here the landlord was only too glad to sell off his scanty supply of whisky to men who were ready to pay five or six pounds for a bottle.

Inevitably the quality of the whisky declined, for few Edinburgh publicans failed to find their own ways of meeting this almost miraculous demand. Adulteration was the usual method of making existing supplies go farther. But there were exceptions. One publican had a stock of 15 under proof whisky of respectable age and sold it pure, at fancy prices, only to Americans. His fame soon spread, and from his house American soldiers walked home with plaited feet. The Scottish soldier, told almost always that the day's supply was finished, raged mightily, and it says much for his restraint that clashes between Scots and Americans were commendably rare and never serious.

If the whisky trade went through somewhat similar vicissitudes during the two world wars, the recovery was much more difficult after the second war. In a financially crippled Britain, a Labour Government, pledged to create the welfare state, sought every means of raising money for this purpose. Whisky was a ready source, for the demand was great and men and women were willing to put their hands into their pockets for what they considered a necessity and the Government taxed as a luxury. The figures speak for themselves. In 1849 the duty per proof gallon of whisky was 3s. 8d. By 1914 it had risen to £1 10s. In 1920 it was raised to £3 12s. 6d. and remained at this figure until 1939. During and since the Second World War it has been raised in a long series of jumps to a stupendous figure. In 1993 a bottle of standard Scotch whisky which, in my youth cost 3s. 6d., sells at £10.80 and of this sum, the Exchequer extorts the astonishing amount of £7.16.

The present effects of this crippling taxation indicate the tendencies and dangers of the future. To help earn badly needed foreign currency after the war, available supplies of Scotch were diverted mainly to exports and it was not until 1960-61, when rationing ended, that home consumption regained its pre-war level of 6.9 million proof gallons. With a larger population and increasing affluence, it would have been reasonable to expect sales to continue to rise steadily but increases in taxes no fewer than 17 times since 1961, have resulted in a fall in Scotch whisky sales in the home market. With no likelihood of any reduction in taxation the prospects of any great increase in home consumption are gloomy. The Government, in fact, seems to regard whisky as a dollar earner abroad and as an evil at home.

Home sales of Scotch whisky rose to a peak of over 52 million proof litres in 1979 but a further nine increases in tax between 1979 and 1993 have had their effect and in 1993 home sales had fallen to 3721 million proof litres, a drop of 18% against 1979. On the other hand, out of US total consumption of whiskies in 1993, that of Scotch whisky amounted to 21% against 15% — the rest being Bourbon and rye.

Fortunately, whereas home sales of Scotch whisky have been damaged by successive Chancellors of the Exchequer, exports of both blended and malt have continued to improve throughout the world. The value of exports in 1993 was more than £2000 million as against £818,000,000 in 1983. In France, for instance, more Scotch whisky is now consumed in a month than of cognac in a year.

Fears of a United States invasion in the form of takeovers of both malt and grain distilleries have, in the main, been proved groundless.

Against today's British price of £10.80 for a standard quality bottle (700cc) of blended Scotch whisky, a similar sized bottle in the US will retail at almost the same price — £10.36 — but bears a far smaller ratio to American wages than does the home price to British wages. Scotch whisky is something more than a mere dollar earner for a Government that is short of dollars. It is a vast industry with markets all over the world. These markets have to be maintained and, if possible, extended, and the price of even the best product must bear some relation to the prices of its rivals.

The superlative merit of Scotch whisky is the fact that it cannot be imitated, and this unique quality comes solely from the richly-flavoured malt whisky of the Highlands. United Distillers is well aware of Highland malt and now owns 31% of the Highland malt whisky distilleries. The proportion of malt whisky in its blended brands may vary, but in general the malt content in exported blended whisky is higher than in bottles marketed in the United Kingdom. It may well be that by its foresight and financial acumen the Distillers Company has saved the Scotch whisky industry, as it assuredly will have to fight for it in the future. But in changing and reducing the original flavour it has created one obvious danger. In a world of uncertainty and strain, more and more people drink in order to give themselves a temporary lift, and both in England and in the United States I have observed that what many men demand of whisky is that it should have no taste and cause no headache.

Distillers throughout the industry must be on their guard against changing and reducing the original flavour of their whiskies, be they blended or malt. The moral for distillers is clearly pointed: so long as the unique qualities of Highland malt can be maintained, so long will the world continue to drink Scotch whisky. The best salesmen of the product are the 20 million or more Scots who today are spread over the face of the earth.

Nevertheless, although there is much truth in the adage that Providence, having given Scotland a bad climate, bestowed on her, by way of compensation, a superlatively good whisky, I cannot deny that change of taste in alcoholic drinks is as inevitable, if not as rapid, as the changes in women's fashions. In England, Scotch whisky drove out brandy as the favourite spirit, and even in my own lifetime Scotch whisky has altered both its flavour and its strength to a remarkable extent. It still retains what I might call its snobbish value, and today I would define the average whisky drinker's attitude towards his favourite drink as a wobble between what he really likes and what he thinks he ought to like.

These changes demand and receive the closest vigilance of the distillers who never relax their efforts to produce better and purer blends. Personally I regret the passing of the single pot-still malt whisky. I drink it whenever I can find it. But I realise that it is the nectar of the young and the strong, that it goes best with Highland air and with long tramps over hill and moor, and that it is ill-suited to the man who sits all day on an office-stool.

Sad, too, is the decrease in the once famous Campbeltown malts which a whisky poetaster eulogises as 'the Hector of the West' and 'deepest-voiced of all the choir'. In Campbeltown there used to be 23 distilleries. Now their whiskies are not in favour for blending, and today only two distilleries are working in this area.

Indeed, it is difficult for anyone with Highland blood in his veins not to feel deep sympathy with the Highland malt distillers. The little man has been swallowed by the big, and, inevitable and financially beneficial as the change may have been, I cannot help feeling that the Highlands, which have suffered so much from neglect for two centuries, have lost another shred of the tattered independence which remains to them. For blending has been the triumph of the Lowlander. Guinness's top management may be in London but its whisky subsidiary, United Distillers, is an Edinburgh company, has its head office in the Scottish capital, and is run mainly by Lowlanders. A hundred and fifty years ago Edinburgh was famous chiefly for its pre-eminence in the law, medicine, letters and the other arts. During the present century its commercial interests have developed so rapidly that now it ranks as one of the great financial cities of the British Empire. This progress is good both for Scotland and for Edinburgh. It would be even more commendable if it had been achieved without detriment to the spirit of Scottish independence and to the prestige of Edinburgh itself, as a truly national capital in which Scottish history and the Scottish arts are not merely dry bones of the past, but living flesh and blood of today.

The visitor to Edinburgh will find much to admire. In particular, he will be grateful to a city which has tended so lovingly the names of its great citizens and has enshrined with such devotion and so much beauty the memory of the Scottish men and women who fought and died for their country. Princes Street, with its array of English multiple shops, may make him rub his eyes, nor will he fail to note that in the centre of the city every second building is a home of finance. In Charlotte Square a neat plaque will indicate to him the mansion in which Field-Marshal Haig was born, but larger lettering will inform him that a bank now occupies the premises, and when he goes to South Castle Street to see the house in which the tireless hand of Scott wrestled to pay off his debts he will find a finance company in possession. What is less likely to catch the visitor's eye is the house in Ellersley Road from which United Distillers exercises control over the malt and grain distilleries it owns in Scotland.

We Scots need to be vigilant that transfer of power to Edinburgh and London does not affect the prosperity of Scotch whisky and continues to provide profitable employment in the Highlands. Change, however, is not necessarily beneficial in itself, and there have been other changes which are wholly deleterious both to the whisky industry and to the Scottish people. The most damaging of these changes have been the incessant numerous rises in taxation which, to an increasing extent, are depriving the Scots of their national drink.

It says much, perhaps too much, for the patience and forbearance of the Scottish people that they have endured this deprivation without violent protest. It requires little effort of the imagination to realise what would happen in France if ever a French Government tried to put wine beyond the reach of the French people. On the contrary, French Governments have always taken the greatest care to ensure that wine shall remain the national drink. Moreover, they have protected cognac, and no brandy, not even that excellent liqueur, Armagnac, can be sold as cognac unless it is made in the Cognac district. In this respect the wise attitude of the French stands out in sharp contrast to the view of the British Government.

I do not doubt that the Scottish people will eventually succeed in restoring whisky to its proper place as the national drink. One thing is certain: the remedy for the existing calamity lies in their hands, and in their hands only. Nor, if the world is spared another war, are the prospects discouraging, for, after years of frustration, decline and neglect, there is now a great and vigorous revival of national sentiment. It is not anti-English. On the contrary, the ties with

England are in some respects stronger than ever. But most Scots, and I would say all Scots who think seriously of their country's future, are resolved that Scotland shall have a larger control of her own national affairs, and of these whisky is certainly one. So strong has this sentiment become that today only differences of opinion regarding the nature and extent of this control divide the nation.

Let the Scottish people therefore raise their voices. Indeed they will be committing suicide if they remain silent, for the choice today is between national revival and a continuation of the anaemic apathy which has already sapped the nation of much of its best blood. But let the voices sound in unison. Plains make for homogeneity, but mountains encourage division, and the tragedy of Scotland has always been her internal rifts and quarrels.

As far as whisky is concerned, no-one wants to see Scotland a drunken country, but surely it is for Scots themselves to decide how much of it they shall drink and what price they shall pay for it. No other race understands better the virtues of moderation. There is, I think, no Scot who does not realise that, if he does not take his whisky, it will sooner or later take him, and to deny him what he has been reared on is an insult both to his intelligence and to his self-respect. The English are ripe in political wisdom, but they do not seem to understand that whisky is part of the Scottish heritage and that, if they continue to tamper with it, they will cause trouble for themselves. For high taxation produces much the same consequences as prohibition, and these are excess, bad liquor, and evasion of the law by illegal distilling.

And the illicit distilling has begun again. During the last war a private still was set up in a shack close to the broad highway in a village not exactly 1000 miles away from that part of the Highlands which I frequent. Indeed, if you were to take away two noughts and then one more you would not be far out in your calculations. The still was like the ramshackle stills of the whisky war of 150 years ago, for the art of distilling is not yet lost. The unconcealable and tell-tale pieces of evidence were the cauldron and the worm, but in the land where beggarly Grants, Chisholms and

Macgregors refused £30,000 for information about the hideout of Prince Charlie, what Highlander would dream of betraying the existence of a private still? And so the still continued faithfully to minister to the just needs of the local population, and its fame spread. Perhaps the fame travelled too far. At any rate the scouts and secret agents of the still reported that the excisemen had got wind of the whisky-making and that a raid might be expected any day.

The elders of the village assembled in council. Detection would have unpleasant consequences, but to destroy a costly cauldron and a cunningly wrought worm would be a sin and a disaster. So that same night a select body of villagers tramped the weary miles to the base of the mountains and gave decent burial to the worm and cauldron at the entrance to one of the passes. Very properly all traces of the burial were obliterated, but its exact whereabouts was carefully recorded by notches on the surrounding trees.

Then came tragedy. When the war was over and whisky was in shorter supply than ever, the villagers returned to the burial ground only to find that the lumberjacks had felled all the trees. Days and nights of search failed to reveal the cauldron and the worm. Later, however, the invisible little folk who dwell at the foot of the Blue Mountains were moved to pity by the sight of so much unrewarded labour and revealed the place to a party of soldiers who were making a road on the very spot.

There were Highlanders in the platoon — decent and well-informed men who knew both the value and the home of what they had found. I have no inkling where the cauldron and worm are today, but I'll stake my last shilling that they are in safe hands and are being kept against the hour when the folly of a London Government becomes too much for Highland honesty. And let me add that in these parts the bus-conductors lay parcels for the farms on bare gateposts anything from 100 to 300 yards away from the house, and that never an article is missing.

Further North there are, I know, other cauldrons and worms kept, not for commercial use, but for the worthy purpose of preventing Scots from being deprived by economic prohibition of their milk. Caithness, however, is not my country, and my lips are sealed. But what a name for a 'local' — The Worm and Cauldron. It would repopulate the Highlands!

When I think of the evils of centralised Government, I always recall a chance meeting with an old Highland shepherd in the autumn of 1947. On my way back from a fishing expedition, my hired car broke down outside a tiny cottage on the Grantown-Tomintoul road. Before the door stood a tall spare man who lent my driver a bicycle and, while the driver went off to get another car, I talked with the man. He was a shepherd, he told me, lived entirely alone and did his own cooking. He must have been well over 70, for he knew all the old people at Balmenach and called my grandmother by her maiden name. He was of course a champion of the past when whisky was cheap and there were no motor cars to drive decent folk and decent beasts off the roads. He recounted with relish great days at the Grantown Cattle Show when Glenlivet and Balmenach flowed freely and all men were equal in their pleasure and came to no harm except a sore head which was soon worked off the next day.

I said to him: 'Well, perhaps it's not such a bad thing that we can't afford to buy whisky any more.' He drew himself up indignantly. 'It's no' only the expense,' he said bitterly, 'it's the scarcity. It's terrible times for Scotland when ye canna buy whisky and oatmeal.'

The weather had now broken and rain had begun to fall. He turned on his heel and excused himself: 'There's a sheep, up the hill yonder that's something wrang wi' it. I maun awa' and see what's ailing.' He called his dogs and away he went.

I watched him for 45 minutes or more until the car came. 'Up the hill' was near the top of one of the lower arms of the Cromdale Hills. Although my sight is good, I could hardly spot a sheep, much less mark one that was ill. But he made great going and, by the time I left, had found his sheep and was a distant speck on the skyline.

Bronzed and erect, he was a fine figure of a man who walked his 20 or 30 miles daily. His bicycle he used for his annual holiday, and the previous year he had cycled the 30 miles from his cottage to Strathdon. The road, hilly almost the whole way, is the highest in Scotland and reaches over 2000ft at the peak point on the Lecht. In order not to lose a precious day of his holiday he cycled through the night and did the trip on whisky and oatmeal, saved and carefully kept for this annual outing.

Whisky and oatmeal! Together with the kilt, the bagpipes and haggis they have been for over a century the butt of comedians and the stock-in-trade of saccharine sentimentalists. Nevertheless, they are the essence of the whole matter, the pattern of the past and the signpost for the future. For if Scotland is to survive as something more than the northern county of England, she must continue to have a culture and life of her own.

She has been in danger of losing both, and whisky and oatmeal are the external symbols of the menace. Oatmeal of a kind has reappeared, but whisky is in mortal peril. On the day when, by long deprivation and desuetude, home Scots cease to drink Scotch whisky, the whole Scottish whisky trade will inevitably decline and other whisky-drinking nations will make their own liquor which, whatever they may choose to call it, will not be Scotch. In a very real sense whisky is the life's blood of the Scot, and I look forward to the day when, among many other things necessary to his survival, he will continue not only to ask for it, but to see that he gets it.

Index